SpringerBriefs in Computer Science

W0079698

For further volumes:
http://www.springer.com/series/10028

Adam Herout · Markéta Dubská
Jiří Havel

Real-Time Detection of Lines and Grids

By PClines and Other Approaches

 Springer

Adam Herout
Department of Computer Graphics
  and Multimedia
Faculty of Information Technology
Brno
Czech Republic

Jiří Havel
Department of Computer Graphics
  and Multimedia
Faculty of Information Technology
Brno
Czech Republic

Markéta Dubská
Department of Computer Graphics
  and Multimedia
Faculty of Information Technology
Brno
Czech Republic

ISSN 2191-5768   ISSN 2191-5776   (electronic)
ISBN 978-1-4471-4413-7   ISBN 978-1-4471-4414-4   (eBook)
DOI 10.1007/978-1-4471-4414-4
Springer London Heidelberg New York Dordrecht

Library of Congress Control Number: 2012944962

Printed on acid-free paper

Springer is part of Springer Science+Business Media (www.springer.com)

Acknowledgement

This work has been supported by the European Regional Development Fund in the "IT4Innovations" Centre of Excellence project (CZ.1.05/1.1.00/02.0070) and by the Ministry of Education, Youth and Sports of the Czech Republic project "Security-Oriented Research in Information Technology", (CEZ MŠMT, MSM0021630528).

Contents

Chapter 1
Introduction

Detection of straight lines is an important basic task of computer vision. It is receiving attention of researchers since the "early days" till today. Solving this task introduced an important concept—the Hough transform. Recently, with the increasing popularity of two dimensional barcodes and augmented reality markers, straight lines are also interesting as a building block of perpendicular grids and chessboard-like structures.

A planar chessboard-like grid is characterized by two groups of lines. Each of the groups of lines has a common vanishing point and, as we discuss in the text, it can be characterized as a whole. A proper representation of such two groups of lines can be used for efficient detection of perpendicular grids. This text deals with suitable representations of grids composed of straight lines and captures the recent development in the Hough transform for straight line detection.

First, Chap. 2 reviews the basics of the Hough transform for line detection. The Hough transform is formalized for 2D curves and some important theoretical properties and relationships to the Radon and Fourier transforms are derived. Chapter 2 also reviews the existing parameterizations of lines which can be used by the Hough transform.

Chapter 3 gives an overview of the existing literature on Hough transform for line detection and it provides a comprehensive overview and taxonomy of the algorithm's variants. The taxonomy is based on a survey article by Kälviäinen et al. [1] but it is updated and extended.

Chapter 4 presents our recent parameterization of lines PClines [2]. This chapter discusses the point-to-line mappings as a class of line parameterizations for the Hough transform. The properties of the point-to-line mappings are further described in Chap. 5 about pencils of lines, regular grids, and possibilities of their detection by the Hough transform.

Chapter 6 presents several efficient implementations of the Hough transform based on the point-to-line-mapping parameterizations. These implementations are using the graphics processors both in the regime of shader computing and in the GPGPU manner. The algorithms presented in this chapter can also be ported to embedded

A. Herout et al., *Real-Time Detection of Lines and Grids*,
SpringerBriefs in Computer Science, DOI: 10.1007/978-1-4471-4414-4_1,
© Adam Herout 2013

processors and reconfigurable chips, because the algorithmic modifications allow for avoiding any floating-point or fractional numbers and they are memory efficient.

References

1. Kälviäinen, H., Hirvonen, P., Xu, L., Oja, E.: Comparisons of probabilistic and non-probabilistic hough transforms. In: Proceedings of 3rd European Conference on Computer Vision ECCV'94, pp. 351–360 (1994)
2. Dubská, M., Herout, A., Havel, J.: PClines—line detection using parallel coordinates. In: Proceedings of CVPR 2011 (2011)

Chapter 2
Review of Hough Transform for Line Detection

This chapter describes the basics of the Hough transform (HT). The terminology to be used in this text is defined in Sects. 2.1 and 2.2. The relationship of the HT (for lines) and the Radon and Fourier transforms is sketched out in Sect. 2.3. Section 2.4 reviews the most common existing line parameterizations used for line detection by the HT and gives a quick comparison of the important ones.

2.1 Hough Transform Basics

The HT [1] is sometimes understood not as a specific algorithm for object detection but as a wide class of algorithms that share a common structure. Princen et al. [2] formalized HT as a *hypothesis testing* process. The structure of HT when described as generically as possible is:

1. Some *evidence* is extracted from the input.
2. For each piece of the evidence, *accumulators* corresponding to the *hypotheses* that are supported by that evidence are incremented. Possible hypotheses are represented by an N-dimensional *parameter space* of accumulators.
3. Probable hypotheses are detected as peaks in the parameter space.

When the HT is used to detect objects in a raster image, the evidence can consist of edge or corner points, local features, and similar. The extracted evidence can be processed completely, or subsampled in a particular way.

The dimensionality of the parameter space is determined by the number of degrees of freedom (DoF) of the hypotheses. The parameter space can be—in the most straightforward manner—represented as an N-dimensional array. The size of the array is determined by the size of the interesting portion of the parameter space and the required precision. It is clear that this representation quickly becomes impractical, as the number of DoF increases. Alternatively, the parameter space can be represented by a linked list or another sparse representation [3].

A. Herout et al., *Real-Time Detection of Lines and Grids*,
SpringerBriefs in Computer Science, DOI: 10.1007/978-1-4471-4414-4_2,
© Adam Herout 2013

The accumulation of the evidence can also be viewed as *voting*. Usually, one piece of evidence affects many hypotheses but only a small portion of the parameter space. The accumulator for each hypothesis is usually (and in the original Hough's form of the transformation) integer, i.e., each piece of the evidence either does or does not support a given hypothesis. However, several variations of HT use fractional accumulators, so that the hypotheses can be supported only partially. Such methods model the parameter space by fuzzy [4] or probabilistic [5] ways or perform some sort of antialiasing [6].

2.2 HT Formalization for 2D Curves

HT is typically used for detecting curves with an analytical description. In that case, the evidence are edge points detected in the input raster image. Such edge points can typically be detected by gradient operators such as Sobel or Prewitt. The hypotheses are the possible curves of a given class in the image. For example, a line has two and a circle has three DoF in a 2D space, but HT can be used for detection of objects such as hyperspheres or hyperplanes in spaces of arbitrary dimensionality.

If a family of (2D) curves is specified by an implicit function

$$f(x, y, p_1, \ldots, p_N) = 0, \tag{2.1}$$

where x and y are the image space coordinates and values $p_1, \ldots, p_N$ the parameter space coordinates, a point (x, y) that lies on a curve specifies a portion of the parameter space that describes all curves passing through this point. The parameter space coordinates and their mapping to the curve specify the *parameterization* of the curve. Curves typically have many possible parameterizations. It is always possible to use a different base if the curve parameters form a vector space, but often, many parameterizations fundamentally different in their nature are usable. Algorithm 1 describes the detection of a curve specified by Eq. (2.1).

In many cases, the edge points are detected by a detector that can estimate the edge orientation (e.g., the Sobel operator). The edge orientation can then be used to reduce the amount of curves that are plausible for the given edge point. Only the accumulators for curves whose tangent direction is close to the direction of the detected edge are incremented. This technique was used by O'Gorman and Clowes [7] to speed up line detection, but it can be used for a wider variety of curves. Various fast HT implementations described in Chaps. 3 and 6 utilize this technique for speeding up the accumulation process.

Shapes that do not have a simple analytical description can be detected by using the Generalized HT by Ballard [8]. In GHT, the object is not described by an equation but by a set of contour elements (edge points). Each contour element is described by its position with respect to the object reference point and the edge orientation. The parameter space has a dimension from two to four (object position, orientation,

---

Algorithm 1 Implicit curve detection by Hough Transform.

Input: Input image I, size of parameter space H
Output: Detected curves C
$\quad P_I = \{(x, y) | (x, y)$ are coordinates of a pixel in I$\}$
$\quad P_H = \{(p_1, \ldots, p_N) | (p_1, \ldots, p_N)$ are coordinates in H$\}$
$\quad H(x) \leftarrow 0, \forall x \in P_H$
$\quad$**for all** $x \in P_I$ **do**
$\quad\quad$**if** at x is an edge in I **then**
$\quad\quad\quad$**for all** $\{p : p \in P_H, f(x, p) = 0\}$ **do**
$\quad\quad\quad\quad H(p) \leftarrow H(p) + 1$
$\quad\quad\quad$**end for**
$\quad\quad$**end if**
$\quad$**end for**
$\quad C = \{p | p \in P_H,$ at p is a high local maximum in $H\}$

---

and scale), but the representation of the detected object is complex even for simple shapes.

The shapes for the GHT can also be expressed by random forests [9]. This representation improves the performance for some kinds of objects. The Hough forests and the HT in general are the alternative of the object detection by a scanning window classifier.

2.3 Hough Transform for Lines and its Relationship to the Radon and Fourier Transform

The HT was originally developed for detecting lines and it is still popular in this particular area. Therefore, a large amount of different line parameterizations and various algorithmic modifications exist. Because 2D lines are rank 1 polynomial functions and therefore have two DoF, all line parameterizations are two dimensional. For now, a line will be specified by its normal vector $\mathbf{n} = (n_x, n_y)$ and the distance from the origin ϱ. Every point $\mathbf{p} = (p_x, p_y)$ that lies on the line fulfills

$$\mathbf{p} \cdot \mathbf{n} = \varrho. \tag{2.2}$$

HT for line detection is closely related to the *Radon Transform* [10, 11]. In the continuous case, these two transforms are identical. They differ in the discrete case, but some of the properties of the Radon transform are still applicable and useful. S.R. Deans [11] examined the properties of the Radon transform of a line segment, a pixel, and a generic curve.

The Radon Transform in an N-dimensional space transforms a function $f : \mathbb{R}^N \to \mathbb{R}$ onto its integrals over hyperplanes. A point $\mathbf{p}$ lies on a hyperplane

$(\mathbf{n}, \varrho)$ iff (if and only if) $\mathbf{p} \cdot \mathbf{n} = \varrho$. The function f must vanish to zero outside of some area around the origin. Otherwise, the value of the line integral would be infinite.

Equation (2.3) differs from the HT structure (Sect. 2.1) in the order of the iteration. The HT iterates over the affected hypotheses for every piece of the evidence so it is building the whole parameter space at once. The RT finds the amount of evidence for a given hypothesis by iterating over the evidence, so it tests every hypothesis separately.

$$
\begin{aligned}
\mathcal{R}^N[f](\mathbf{n}, \varrho) &= \int_{\mathbb{R}^N} f(\mathbf{x})\delta(\mathbf{x} \cdot \mathbf{n} - \varrho)d\mathbf{x} \\
&= \int_{\mathbf{x}\cdot\mathbf{n}=\varrho} f(\mathbf{x})d\mathbf{x} \\
&= \int_{\mathbf{n}^\perp} f(\varrho\mathbf{n} + \mathbf{x})d\mathbf{x}
\end{aligned}
\tag{2.3}
$$

Through the relation to the Radon Transform, the HT is also related to the Fourier Transform. One- and N-dimensional versions of the Fourier transform are

$$
\mathcal{F}^1[f](\xi) = \int_{-\infty}^{\infty} f(x)e^{-2\pi i x\xi}dx,
\tag{2.4}
$$

$$
\mathcal{F}^N[f](\mathbf{w}) = \int_{\mathbb{R}^N} f(\mathbf{x})e^{-2\pi i(\mathbf{x}\cdot\mathbf{w})}d\mathbf{x}.
\tag{2.5}
$$

The transforms are related via the Projection-Slice theorem [10], where the Radon transform is the projection part. One-dimensional Fourier transform of the Radon transform is equal to a slice of the N-dimensional Fourier transform along the direction specified by the hyperplane's normal vector. Notation

$$
\mathcal{R}^N[f](\mathbf{n}, \varrho) = \mathcal{R}_{\mathbf{n}}^N[f](\varrho)
\tag{2.6}
$$

will be used. The relation between Radon and Fourier transform is then

$$
\mathcal{F}^1[\mathcal{R}_{\mathbf{n}}^N[f]](\xi) = \mathcal{F}^N[f](\xi\mathbf{n}).
\tag{2.7}
$$

Due to this relation, 2D convolution in the image space can be transformed to 1D convolution in the parameter space as

$$
\mathcal{R}_{\mathbf{n}}^N[f * g](\varrho) = (\mathcal{R}_{\mathbf{n}}^N[f] * \mathcal{R}_{\mathbf{n}}^N[g])(\varrho).
\tag{2.8}
$$

The proof can be found in the work of Natterer [10]. This feature can be used not only for image filtering, but it also generalizes the technique Han et al. used for calculation of the α-cut in the Fuzzy HT [4].

Moving the filtering from the image to the parameter space can be beneficial not only because of the lower computational cost. For example, some filtering methods can interfere with the edge detection and moving the filtering after the voting step (to the voting space) allows for filtering without disturbing the edge detection phase.

2.4 Line Parameterizations

Usage of the HT for line parameterization requires a point transformation to the Hough space. The motivation for introducing new parameterizations is to find the optimal trade-off between requirements for the transformation. These requirements include preference of bounding Hough space, discretization with minimal aliasing errors, and uniform distribution of discretization error or intuitive mapping from original system to the Hough space. In general, the image of a point can be a curve of different shapes; for example circle, sinusoid curve, straight line, etc.

A subset favoring intuitive mapping and very fast line rasterization is the set of *point-to-line mappings* (PTLM). It contains such parameterizations where a point in the source image corresponds to a line in the Hough space and—naturally for the HT—a point in the Hough space represents a line in the x-y image space. PTLM were studied by Bhattacharya et al. [12], who proved that for a single PTLM, the Hough space must be infinite. However, for many PTLMs, a complementary PTLM can be found, so that the two mappings define two finite Hough spaces containing all lines possible in the bounded image. An example is the original HT (Eq. 2.14) which uses one Hough space for the vertical lines and the second one for the horizontal lines.

The following text will first present transformations based on 'classic' line parameterizations and the representations of these parameters. The second half belongs to the parameterizations using values of intersections of the line and a bounding object. At the end of this section, a comparison of the mentioned parameterizations is made, focusing on utilization of the Hough space and its main characteristics.

Slope–Intercept Parameterization
The first HT, introduced and patented by Paul Hough in 1962 [1], was based on the line equation in the slope-intercept form. However, the exact line equation is not mentioned in the patent itself. Commonly, the slope-intercept line equation has the form:

$$\ell : y = xm + b, \tag{2.9}$$

but the method used in the Hough's patent corresponds to the parameterization:

$$\ell : x = ym + b. \tag{2.10}$$

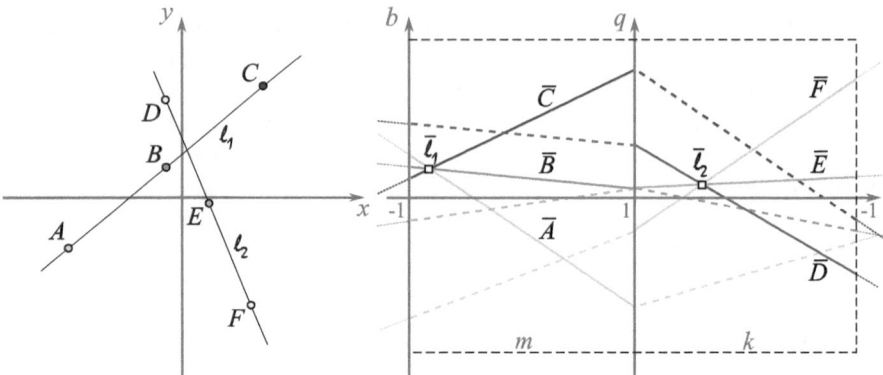

Fig. 2.1: Hough transform using m–b and k–q parameterizations of a line. *Left* input image; *right* corresponding Hough space

Using parameters m and b, all lines passing through a single point form a line in the Hough space, so it is a PTLM. As in every PTLM, the parameter space of all possible lines in a bounded input image is infinite [12]. Using a bounded parameter space requires at least two complementary spaces of parameters. In the case of the slope–intercept line equation, these spaces are, for example, the two based on these equations (Fig. 2.1):

$$y = xm + b,$$
$$x = yk + q. \tag{2.11}$$

The slope–intercept parameterization is one of the parameterizations that allows for moving the image convolution to the parameter space as shown in Sect. 2.3. Contrary to Eq. (2.8), some scaling is necessary.

$$\mathcal{H}_m[f * g](b) = \frac{1}{\sqrt{1 + m^2}} (\mathcal{H}_m[f] * \mathcal{H}_m[g])(b). \tag{2.12}$$

Cascaded Hough Transform

Tuytelaars et al. [13] added a third space and used this three-fold parameterization to detect the vanishing points and the horizon. This modification, named *Cascaded Hough Transform*, uses three pairs of parameters based on Eq. (2.13).

$$ax + b + y = 0 \tag{2.13}$$

The three subspaces are created as shown in Fig. 2.2. The first one has coordinates a–b, the second $(1/a)$–(b/a), and the third $(1/b)$–(a/b). All spaces are restricted to the interval $[-1, 1]$ in both directions. Each point (x, y) in the original space is transformed into a line in each of the three subspaces. Moreover, even in an

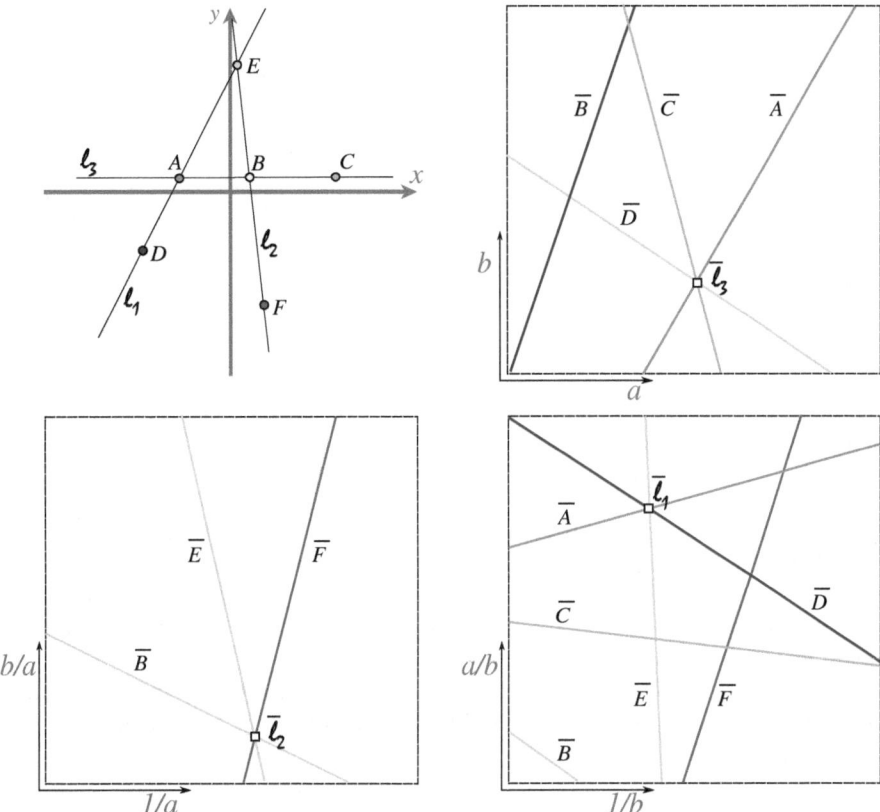

Fig. 2.2: Cascaded Hough transform using three spaces. *Left-top* input image; *Right* and *Bottom* corresponding Hough spaces

unbounded image plane, every line corresponds to a point with coordinates within area $[-1, 1] \times [-1, 1]$ for one of the spaces (see Fig. 2.2).

Consider the input image scaled to get image boundaries ± 1. The significant part of the third subspace is without any vote and just the first two subspaces are needed to represent all lines from the image. However, CHT is mainly used for vanishing points and line detection, where the third space is indispensable. For more details, please see [13, 14].

$\theta - \varrho$ parameterization

In 1972, Duda and Hart [15] introduced a very popular parameterization denoted as $\theta - \varrho$ which is very important for its inherently bounded parameter space. It is based on the line equation in the normal form (2.14)

$$y \sin \theta + x \cos \theta = \varrho, \tag{2.14}$$

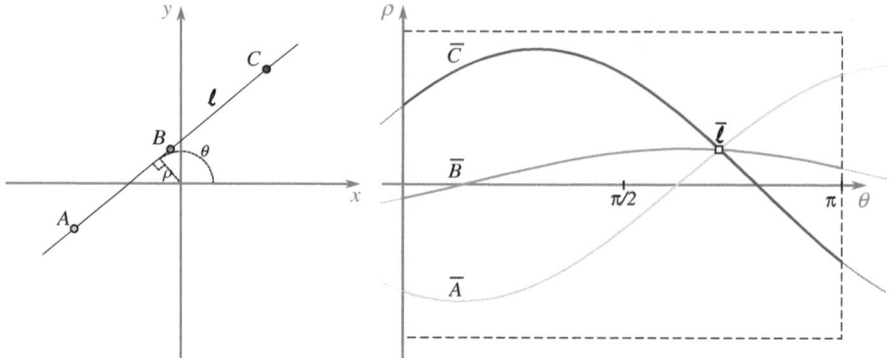

Fig. 2.3: Hough transform using $\theta - \varrho$ parameterization of line. *Left* input space; *right* corresponding Hough space

where parameter θ represents the angle of inclination and ϱ is the length of the shortest chord between the line and the origin of the image coordinate system (Fig. 2.3 left). In this case, images of all lines passing through a single point form a sinusoid curve in the parameter space (Fig. 2.3 right). Hence, $\theta - \varrho$ is not a PTLM and for a bounded input image it has a bounded parameter space.

For the $\theta - \varrho$ parameterization, Eq. (2.8) can be used without any modification. Therefore, an image convolution (filtering) can be done by a 1D convolution of the Hough space of image f with kernel g as

$$\mathcal{H}_\theta[f * g](\varrho) = (\mathcal{H}_\theta[f] * \mathcal{H}_\theta[g])(\varrho). \tag{2.15}$$

Circle Transform

Similar to the $\theta - \rho$ parameterization, the *circle transform* [16] uses the normal equation of the line (2.14). However, instead of the θ and ρ parameters it uses the intersection of the line and its normal passing through the origin O. This point fully characterizes a line. From the other side, points corresponding to all possible lines passing through an arbitrary point create a circle (see Fig. 2.4), i.e., point P is by the CT transformed into circle $\mathbf{c}$. The center of the circle $\mathbf{c}$ is the midpoint between O and P and the radius is equal to one-half of the distance $|OP|$ (Eq. 2.16).

$$P = (a, b)_{\mathbb{E}^2} = (\rho \cos \theta, \rho \sin \theta)$$
$$\mathbf{c} : x = \frac{1}{2}(\rho \cos \theta + O_x) \tag{2.16}$$
$$y = \frac{1}{2}(\rho \sin \theta + O_y)$$

The problem of such accumulation is that at the origin and very close to it, the number of votes is much higher than in the rest of the accumulator space. It is because

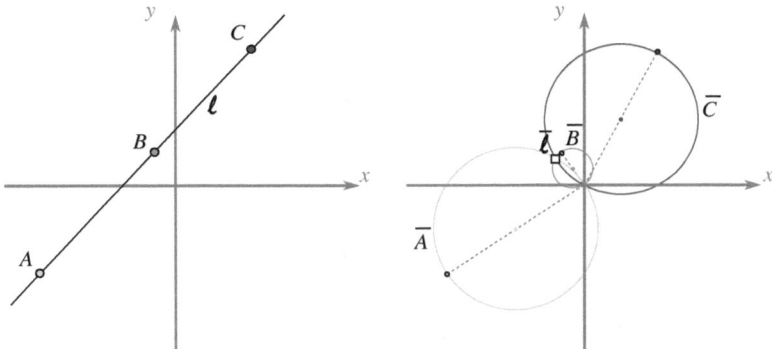

Fig. 2.4: Circle transform using θ–ϱ parameterization of line. *Left* input space; *right* corresponding Hough space

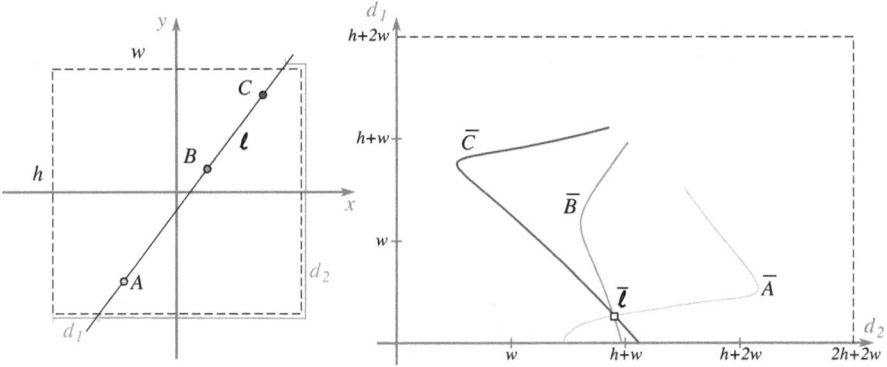

Fig. 2.5: Muff Transform. A line is parameterized by its intersections with the bounding rectangle

all circles pass through the origin by definition. The possible solution is to put the origin outside of the input image. However, the usage of the second space is needed because some line representations can now also lie outside of the input image.

Muff Transform

Several research groups invested effort to find other bounded parameterizations suitable for the HT. One of them is the *Muff-transform* introduced by Wallace in 1985 [17] (Fig. 2.5). As the basis for this parameterization, a bounding rectangle around the image is used. Each line intersects the bounding box at exactly two points. The distance of the first intersection (i.e. the nearest intersection from the origin along the perimeter) on the perimeter from the origin, and the distance between the first and the second intersections are used as the parameters.

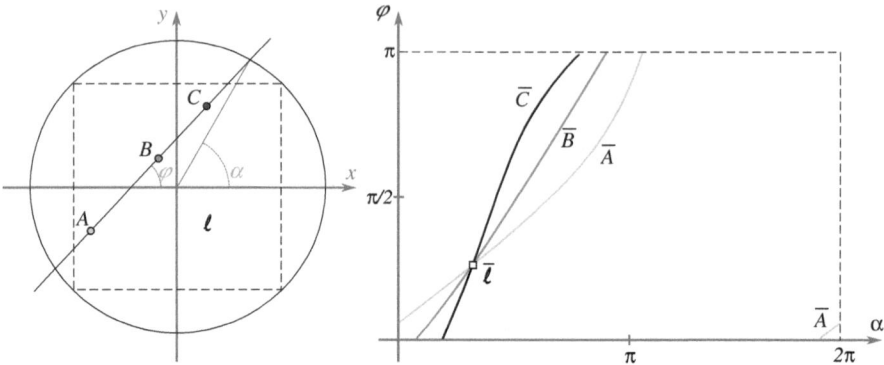

Fig. 2.6: Fan-Beam Transform. Line is parametrized by its orientation and intersection with the bounding circle

The main advantages are the bounded Hough space and the discretization error connected directly to the discretization of the input image; thus, it is possible to represent all necessary values as integers. The problem is the very sparse usage of the Hough space. However, this can be eliminated by rearrangement of the components of the accumulator space. Also, the curve accumulated to the space has discontinuities caused by corners of the bounding rectangle.

Fan–Beam Parameterization

Using a circle instead of a rectangle defines another bounded parameterization, called the *fan–beam* parameterization [10] (Fig. 2.6). Again, a line and a circle intersect at exactly two points. Angles defined by these two points were used for a line parameterization for the first time by Eckhardt and Maderlechner [18].

Similar to Muff transform, the parameters belong to the original image plane which makes the discretization intuitive. In contrast, the accumulated line is smooth, and the aliasing error is thus minimized. The accumulator, again, needs rearrangement for optimal utilization of the memory.

Forman Transform

The Muff transform is also a basis for a parameterization introduced by Forman [19], who combined it with $\theta - \varrho$ and represented lines by the first intersection point and the line's orientation θ (Fig. 2.7).

2.4.1 A Quick Comparison of Selected Line Parameterizations

Different line parameterizations offer advantages and each one of them has its costs. One important aspect of the parameterizations' properties is the uniformity of sampling of the voting space. The behavior of different parameterizations is illustrated by images in Fig. 2.8.

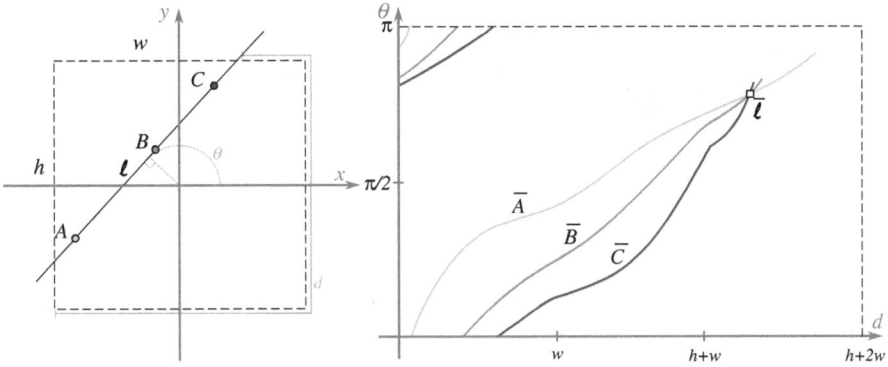

Fig. 2.7: Forman's parameterization based on $\theta-\varrho$ and Muff Transform

Figure 2.8 shows the utilization of the Hough space for different parameterizations in a manner similar to the work of Mejdani et al. [20]. The Hough space is accumulated for a 128×128 square image with each point considered as an edge point for accumulation (left column) and for an image with four lines (right column). The more the votes are accumulated, the darker the color is used. Always, the point with a maximal number of votes has absolutely black color and the point with the lowest value is white. Between these values, the color is linearly interpolated depending on the number of votes.

It should be noted that each parameterization can have an accumulator space a little bit different for different implementations, for example when the origin is in the center of the input image or in its corner. Some of the parameterizations have the accumulator space composed from several subspaces, which also enables a better arrangement for optimal utilization of computer memory. However, the arrangement used in Fig. 2.8 is sufficient for the illustration and corresponds to Figs. 2.1–2.7.

From the rasterized Hough spaces, several characteristic aspects can be observed. The main is the utilization of the accumulator (Table 2.1). The best utilization has the PClines parameterization (Chap. 4); on the other hand, the largest unused parts has the Fan beam transform. The second is the distribution of the votes and the number of bins with the maximal value. In an ideal case, one bin in the accumulator space corresponds to one line in the input image. This implies that the maximum of the votes has to be equal to the length (number of pixels) of the longest line in the image. Such a line is the diagonal and it occurs two times in the rectangular shape. That means two bins with maximal votes. A higher number of maximal bins, for example in the slope-intercept parameterization, indicates the presence of aliasing errors caused by discretization.

Different transformations also vary in the rasterized and accumulated shape in the Hough space. From computational aspect, the fastest is accumulation of lines. However, as mentioned at the beginning of this section and proved in [12], all PTLM need at least two twin spaces. This causes discontinuities and (dis)favors lines with

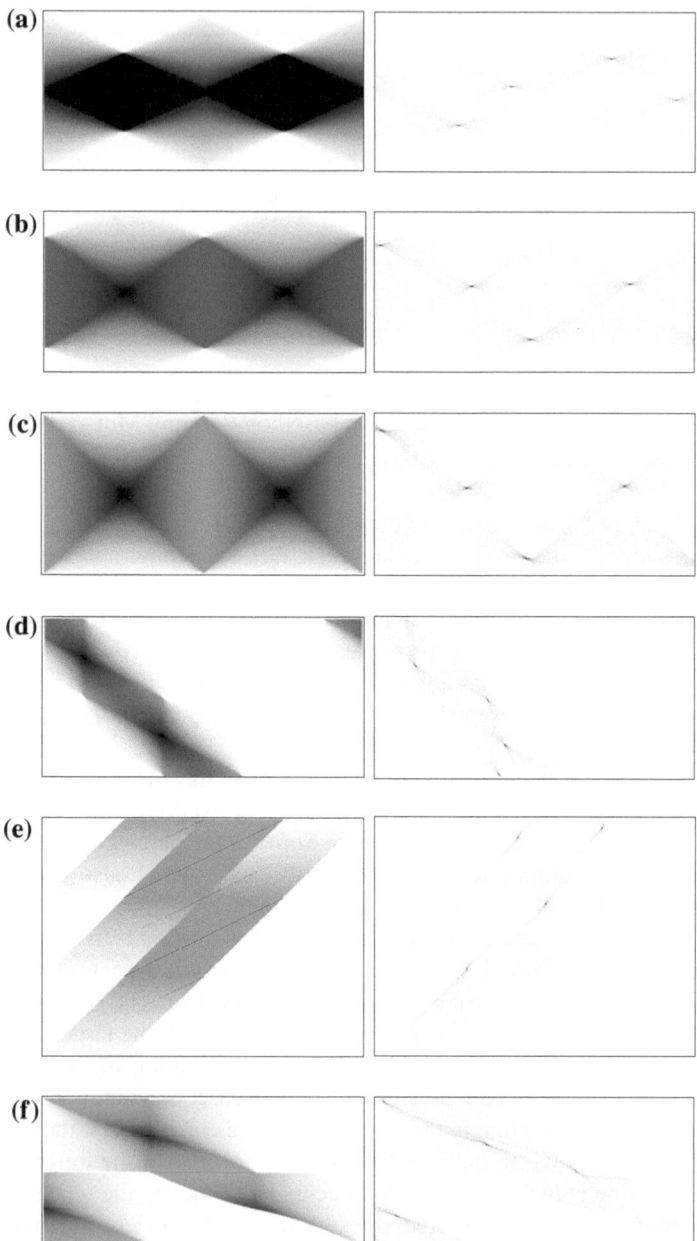

Fig. 2.8: **a** Slope-intercept parameterization; **b** $\theta-\varrho$ parameterization; **c** PClines (see Chap. 4); **d** fan-beam parameterization; **e** Muff transform; **f** Forman transform

Table 2.1: Basic characteristics of the selected transformations

	Parameterization	Utilization (%)	Image of a point	Space components
slope–intercept	Slope–intercept	75	Lines	2
$\theta - \varrho$	Inclination–distance	89	Sinusoid curve	1
Cascaded	Slope–intercept	–	Lines	3
Circle	Inclination–distance	–	Circle	2
PClines	xy coordinate	100	Lines	1
Muff	Bounding rectangle	50	Curve	6
Fan–beam	Bounding circle	36	Curve	1
Forman	Inclination–distance Bounding box	63	Curve	1

The first column reflects the used parameters/values; the second is the fraction of the bins from the Hough space where at least one vote is present; the third is the shape of the image of a point after mapping; and the last is the number of components in which the Hough space can be divided canonically

specific orientations. For example, when using the $\theta - \varrho$ transformation, a point is mapped to a smooth sinusoid curve and the discretization error is distributed uniformly through the whole Hough space. On the other hand, a PTLM slope–intercept parameterization prefers diagonal lines over horizontal and vertical (for more information about the discretization error, please see Sect. 4.3). The types of point images for different parameterizations are concluded in Table 2.1.

The last property shown in Table 2.1 is the number of components of the Hough space. This reflects the number of subspaces required, for example, from the definition of the PTLMs. The value also serves as information of discontinuity of the whole space. The higher the number is, the more the joints are in the space which implies more discontinuities.

References

1. Hough, P.V.C.: Method and means for recognizing complex patterns. U.S. Patent 3,069,654, 1962
2. Princen, J., Illingowrth, J., Kittler, J.: Hypothesis testing: a framework for analyzing and optimizing Hough transform performance. IEEE Trans. Pattern Anal. Mach. Intell. 16(4), 329–341 (1994). http://dx.doi.org/10.1109/34.277588
3. Kälviäinen, H., Hirvonen, P., Xu, L., Oja, E.: Probabilistic and non-probabilistic Hough transforms: overview and comparisons. Image Vis. Comput. 13(4), 239–252 (1995). doi:10.1016/0262-8856(95)99713-B, http://www.sciencedirect.com/science/article/pii/026288569599713B
4. Han, J.H., Kóczy, L.T., Poston, T.: Fuzzy Hough transform. Pattern Recogn. Lett. 15, 649–658 (1994). doi:10.1016/0167-8655(94)90068-X, http://dl.acm.org/citation.cfm?id=189757.189759
5. Stephens, R.: Probabilistic approach to the Hough transform. Image Vis. Comput. 9(1), 66–71 (1991). doi:10.1016/0262-8856(91)90051-P, http://www.sciencedirect.com/science/article/pii/026288569190051P

6. Kiryati, N., Bruckstein, A.: Antialiasing the Hough transform. CVGIP Graph. Models Image Process. **53**(3), 213–222 (1991). doi:10.1016/1049-9652(91)90043-J, http://www.sciencedirect.com/science/article/pii/104996529190043J
7. O'Gorman, F., Clowes, M.B.: Finding picture edges through collinearity of feature points. IEEE Trans. Comput. **25**(4), 449–456 (1976)
8. Ballard, D.H.: Generalizing the Hough transform to detect arbitrary shapes. Pattern Recogn. **13**(2), 111–122 (1981)
9. Gall, J., Yao, A., Razavi, N., Gool, L.V., Lempitsky, V.: Hough forests for object detection, tracking, and action recognition. IEEE Trans. Pattern Anal. Mach. Intell. **33**, 2188–2202 (2011). http://doi.ieeecomputersociety.org/10.1109/TPAMI.2011.70
10. Natterer, F.: The Mathematics of Computerized Tomography. Wiley, New York (1986)
11. Deans, S.R.: Hough transform from the radon transform. IEEE Trans. Pattern Anal. Mach. Intell. **PAMI-3**(2), 185–188 (1981). doi:10.1109/TPAMI.1981.4767076
12. Bhattacharya, P., Rosenfeld, A., Weiss, I.: Point-to-line mappings as Hough transforms. Pattern Recogn. Lett. **23**(14), 1705–1710 (2002). http://dx.doi.org/10.1016/S0167-8655(02)00133-2
13. Tuytelaars, T., Proesmans, M., Gool, L.V., Mi, E.: The cascaded hough transform. In: Proceedings of ICIP, pp. 736–739 (1997)
14. Tuytelaars, T., Proesmans, M., Gool, L.V.: The cascaded Hough transform as support for grouping and finding vanishing points and lines. In: Proceedings of the International Workshop on Algebraic Frames for the Perception-Action Cycle, AFPAC '97, pp. 278–289. Springer, London, UK (1997). http://dl.acm.org/citation.cfm?id=646049.677093
15. Duda, R.O., Hart, P.E.: Use of the Hough transformation to detect lines and curves in pictures. Commun. ACM **15**(1), 11–15 (1972). http://doi.acm.org/10.1145/361237.361242
16. Sewisy, A.A.: Graphical techniques for detecting lines with the hough transform. Int. J. Comput. Math. **79**(1), 49–64 (2002). doi:10.1080/00207160211911, http://www.tandfonline.com/doi/abs/10.1080/00207160211911
17. Wallace, R.: A modified Hough transform for lines. In: Proceedings of CVPR 1985, pp. 665–667 (1985)
18. Eckhardt, U., Maderlechner, G.: Application of the projected Hough transform in picture processing. In: Proceedings of the 4th International Conference on Pattern Recognition, pp. 370–379. Springer, London, UK (1988)
19. Forman, A.V.: A modified Hough transform for detecting lines in digital imagery. Appl. Artif. Intell. **III**, 151–160 (1986)
20. El Mejdani, S., Egli, R., Dubeau, F.: Old and new straight-line detectors: description and comparison. Pattern Recogn. **41**, 1845–1866 (2008). doi:10.1016/j.patcog.2007.11.013, http://dl.acm.org/citation.cfm?id=1343128.1343451

Chapter 3
Variants of the Hough Transform for Straight Line Detection

Various research groups invested effort to deal with computational complexity of the Hough transform and/or to improve the accuracy of the detection. Different methods focus on special data structures, non-uniform resolution of the accumulation array, special rules for picking points from the input image, or they employ specialized hardware units, etc.

In the following text, these methods are divided into three categories. To be consistent with existing notation, two groups are made similar to ones defined and used by Kälviäinen et al. [1]. The first group, named *non-probabilistic*, includes the *standard hough transform* (SHT) [2] and its modifications [3] which use all edge points from the input image. Methods based on the random sampling using just a subset of the edge points belong the to second category—*probabilistic* Hough transforms. The most significant representative of this group is the *randomized hough transform* (RHT) [4]. This division might be confusing since to the *non-probabilistic* methods belongs, among others, the *probabilistic hough transform* (ProbHT) [5]. To clarify, the property of being probabilistic of the HT methods relates to the way in which the edge points are picked from the set, while in the ProbHT the accumulators represent the probability of the line, not just the number of the voting edges.

The last category includes implementations using special hardware, such as embedded systems or GPU architectures. Methods implemented on these systems are in most cases based on methods from one of the first two groups. We mention these approaches here to show how to deal with HT bottlenecks in such a way which takes into account the hardware features and limitations.

Probabilistic and non-probabilistic methods are classified according to three criteria:

Mapping specifies how many image points produce groups of parameter space points and how large these groups are. For example, the "normal" Hough transform is one-to-many, because it rasterizes the whole curve from only one image point.

Accumulator specifies the data structure used for the accumulator.

Detection distinguishes whether the method detects each line separately, or all lines in the image (almost) simultaneously.

A. Herout et al., *Real-Time Detection of Lines and Grids*,
SpringerBriefs in Computer Science, DOI: 10.1007/978-1-4471-4414-4_3,
© Adam Herout 2013

The following Sects. 3.1 and 3.2 give a detailed overview of efficient variants of the Hough transform for line detection. For a concise overview of the basic characteristics of the mentioned methods, please refer to Tables 3.1 and 3.2 on pages 19 and 20.

3.1 Non-probabilistic Methods

Let us briefly recall and summarize the SHT [2, 3] algorithm discussed in detail in Sect. 2.1. It consists of three parts:

1. *Accumalation* of a curve in the Hough space for each edge point.
2. *Finding the local maxima* in the space.
3. *Extracting line segments* corresponding to the positions of the local maxima (Algorithm 2).

Algorithm 2 HT for detecting line segments based on the $\theta-\varrho$ parameterization.

Require: Input image I with dimensions I_w, I_h, Hough space dimensions H_ϱ, H_θ
Ensure: Detected lines segments $L = \{\ell_1, \ldots\}$
1: $H(\bar{\varrho}, \bar{\theta}) \leftarrow 0, \forall \bar{\varrho} \in \{1, \ldots, H_\varrho\}, \bar{\theta} \in \{1, \ldots, H_\theta\}$
2: **for all** $x \in \{1, \ldots, I_w\}, y \in \{1, \ldots, I_h\}$ **do**
3:    **if** $I(x, y)$ **is edge then**
4:       **increment** $H(\bar{\varrho}(\bar{\theta}, x, y), \bar{\theta}), \forall \bar{\theta} \in \{1, \ldots, H_\theta\}$
5:    **end if**
6: **end for**
7: $L' = \{(\theta(\bar{\theta}), \varrho(\bar{\varrho})) | \bar{\varrho} \in \{1, \ldots, H_\varrho\} \wedge \bar{\theta} \in \{1, \ldots H_\theta\} \wedge$ at $(\bar{\varrho}, \bar{\theta})$ is a local maximum in H above a threshold$\}$
8: **for all** $(\theta, \varrho) \in L'$ **do**
9:    **find line segment** ℓ_i
10:    $L = L \cup \ell_i$
11: **end for**

The main bottlenecks of this approach are its computational complexity and storage requirements. Another problem is the accuracy of the object detection, which is sensitive to the resolution of the accumulator space and to the noise in the image.

Various modifications of the SHT algorithm aim at solving some of the bottlenecks or limitations of the algorithm. In the following text, *non-probabilistic* modifications of the SHT are discussed in the chronological order from the oldest to the present methods.

The first attempts to solve the storage problem were proposed by Li et al. in their modification named *fast hough transform* (FHT) [6] and by Illingworth and Kittler in *adaptive hough transform* (AHT) [7]. Both, FHT and AHT, used an iterative exploration of the accumulation space. The idea of the FHT is to recursively divide the space into hypercubes from low to high resolution. Only the hypercubes with the number of votes over a given threshold T are processed again. This subdivision continues until the hypercube reaches a predefined size or its score is lower then T.

Table 3.1 Overview of the Hough transform variants for straight line detection. This is an update of the survey by Kälviäinen et al. [1]

Method	Mapping	Accumulator	Detection
Non-probabilistic hough transforms			
SHT	One-to-many	2D array	All lines
FHT	One-to-many	2 × 2D quadtree	All lines
AHT	One-to-many	2 × small 2D array	Line by line
AnHT	One-to-many	2D array	All lines
HHT	One-to-many	varying sized 2D arrays + 2D linked list	Line by line
CHT	Many-to-one	2D array	All lines
CFHT	Many-to-one	2D linked list	All lines
PHT	One-to-many	2D array	All lines
MRHT	One-to-many	varying sized 2D arrays	All lines
SaHT	One-to-many	2D array	All lines
HKHT	One-to-one	2×2D array	All lines
CnsHT	Many-to-one	1D array	Line by line
MHT	Many-to-one	1D array + linked list	Line by line
PAAHT	One-to-many	1D array	Line by line
EPHT	One-to-many	2D array	All lines
THT	One-to-many	2D array	All lines
GrHT	Many-to-one	2D linked list	All lines
EHT	One-to-many	2 × 3D array	All lines
	Many-to-one		
RegHT	One-to-many	2D array	All lines
NUHT	One-to-many	2D array	All lines
IVHT	Many-to-one	2D array	All lines
StHT	–	2D array	All lines
SSHT	One-to-many	2D array	All lines
IHT	Many-to-one	small 2D array	Line by line
Probabilistic hough transforms			
Method	Mapping	Accumulator	Detection
RHT	Many-to-one	2D linked list	Line by line
WRHT	Many-to-one	2D linked list	Line by line
RWRHT	Many-to-one	2D linked list	Line by line
MSHT	Many-to-one	2D array	All lines
CRHT	Many-to-one	2D linked list	Line by line
DRHT	Many-to-one	2D linked list	Line by line
DCHT	Many-to-one	θ-histogram	Line by line
ProbHT	One-to-many	2D array	All lines
MCHT	All	2D array	All lines
ConHT	Many-to-one	2 × 1D θ-accumulator	Line by line
PPHT	One-to-many	2D array	Line by line
BHT	Many-to-one	–	Line by line
ISHT	–	2D array	Line by line
NPHT	Many-to-one	2D linked list	Line by line

SHT	Standard hough transform [3]
FHT	Fast hough transform [6]
AHR	Adaptive hough transform [7]
AnHT	Antialiasing the hough transform [9]
HHT	Hierarchical hough transform [10]
CHT	Combinatorial hough transform [11]
CFHT	Curve fitting hough transform [12]
PHT	Probabilistic hough transform by Stephens [13]
MRHT	Multiresolution hough transform [14]
CnsHT	Constrained hough transform [17]
MHT	Modified hough transform [18]
PAAHT	HT with principal axis analysis [20]
THT	Thickness hough transform [23]
EHT	Extended hough transform [24]
RegHT	Regularized hough transform [25]
NUHT	Nonuniform hough transform [26]
StHT	Statistical hough transform [28]
SSHT	Hough transform with surround suppression voting scheme [29]
DCHT	Dynamic combinatorial hough transform [11]
RHT	Randomized hough transform [4]
ProbHT	Probabilistic hough transform by Kiryati [5]
MCHT	Monte carlo hough transform [35]
SaHT	Sampling hough transform [15]
HKHT	Hough transform with 2D hypothesis testing kernel [16]
ConHT	Connective hough transform [36]
WRHT	Window randomized hough transform [30]
RWRHT	Random window randomized hough transform [30]
CRHT	Connective randomized hough transform [32]
DRHT	Dynamic randomized hough transform [33]
PPHT	Progressive probabilistic hough transform [37]
EPHT	Error propagation for the hough transform (EPHT) [19]
BHT	Hough transform using belt voting [39]
ISHT	Importance sampling hough transform [40]
EPRHT	Randomised hough transform with error propagation [41]
GrHT	Gridding hough transform [22]
MSHT	Mean-shift hough transform [31]
IVHT	Improved voting hough transform [27]
NpHT	N-Point hough transform [34]
IHT	Improved hough transform [43]

The final hypercubes are used for selection of the peaks. The main benefit of this approach is the reduction of storage requirements and straightforward parallelization of the algorithm. The parameters used in the FHT, like threshold T or position and size of subsequent windows are fixed. This can cause problems, for example, if a peak is near to a border of a hypercube.

The AHT handles these situations be making the parameters flexible. At each resolution, the parameter space is analyzed and more appropriate parameters are defined. In comparison with FHT, the disadvantage is that objects (lines,circles, ...) are searched one by one and for finding more instances, the algorithm has to be reinitialized and repeated.

The accuracy of the HT is strongly dependent on the detection of maxima in the parameter space. Two new methods for peak detection were presented by Niblack and Petkovic [8]. Both methods use preprocessing and interpolation in the Hough space, and they are based on compensating for effects that cause spreading of the peak in the Hough space. The first method uses a sliding rectangular window and the main idea is to iteratively find the maximal sum in a subwindow. The second method used a Gaussian window instead of the rectangular one.

Improving the Hough Transform in the stage of accumulation can be done by *antialising the hough transform* (AnHT) [9]. It has been proven that the accumulator method implies sampling of a non-bandlimited signal. This results in aliasing difficulties in the algorithm. In the work of Kiryati and Bruckstein, the sampling requirements based on the sampling theorem are presented and related to the effective bandwidth of the extended HT. The relation between the number of accumulators and the performance has been also clarified.

To accumulate the edge points from small subimages is the main idea of the *hierarchical hough transform* (HHT) [10]. The algorithm is designed particularly for the straight line detection. First, the complete image is divided into a number of subimages and the Hough transform is performed separately on each of them. The detected line segments form the bottom level of a pyramid structure. By grouping these segments and propagating them up in the hierarchy, the longer lines are obtained. The result of this approach is a hierarchical description of the line segments in the image. HHT is suitable for parallel processing and since the algorithm is executing the SHT on the small images, the accumulator space can be kept small.

Based on the idea that a line is uniquely defined by two points, Ben-Tzvi proposed the *combinatorial hough transform* (CHT) [11]. Each pair of the edge pixels determines the line parameters (θ and ρ) and just one corresponding cell in the accumulator array is increased. To avoid accumulation of the huge amount of all possible pairs, the input image is divided into subregions and pairs are searched within one common segment. Accumulation of just one point instead of accumulating the whole curve makes maxima more significant and thus the extraction of parameters is easier and more precise. The method is suitable for sparse images where the CHT is more efficient than the SHT.

A method suitable for detection of curves with an arbitrary parameter range characterized by small storage requirements was introduced by Liang as the so-called *curve fitting hough transform* (CFHT) [12]. First, a segment of a curve is fitted to a small neighborhood of previously detected edge points. The fitting error is evaluated and if it is smaller than a given threshold, the parameters of the fitted curve are derived. These parameters, again, define one point in the parameter space. Instead of storing the whole array, a multidimensional ordered parameter list is used. This leads to lower storage requirements and computational speed-up.

The relationship between the Hough transform and the Maximum Likelihood method was shown by Stephens and it is widely known as the *probabilistic hough transform* (PHT) [13]. In contrast to previous variants of the HT, which are defined algorithmically and operate on discrete spaces, the PHT is defined as a continuous mathematical function. PHT can be applied to a wide range of problems from simple straightline detection to high-dimensional problems such as object tracking. This approach brings accurate results, but it is computationally expensive.

A modification similar to FHT and AHT based on coarse-to-fine iterative search is the *multiresolution hough transform* (MRHT) by Atiquzzaman [14]. The differences are in usage of multiresolution images and accumulator arrays, a logarithmic parameter-range reduction method for faster convergence, and consideration of the discretization errors. The MHT exploits the reduced information content of multiresolution images and accumulator arrays at the different iterations. First, a set of reduced-resolution images are generated from the original image. The HT is first applied to the smallest image using a very small accumulator array and subsequent iterations use images and accumulators of increasing size.

In order to reduce the computation time, a simple sampling technique was proposed—the *sampling hough transform* (SaHT) [15]. In the SaHT algorithm, the image is first divided into 3×3 subregions. For each subregion, only one pixel is evaluated by using the Sobel operator. The position of the selected pixels is fixed and depends on the position of the subregion. When the gradient magnitude of the pixel is greater than a predefined threshold, the other eight pixels from the subregion are also processed by the edge detector and mapped to the parameter space. If it is smaller, the subregion is considered as an edge-free region. The computation time is reduced compared to the SHT, but the detection rate remains similar.

Palmer et al. introduced a line finding algorithm based on the Hough transform in which the voting kernel is a smooth function of differences in both of the line parameters—the *hough transform with 2D hypothesis testing kernel* (HKHT) [16]. The algorithm uses a hypothesis testing where each cell of the Hough space represents a hypothetical line that runs through the image. The two-dimensional kernel depends on the distance of the pixel from the hypothetical line and on the difference between the orientation of the local edge (found by the edge detector) and the orientation of the hypothetical line.

Olson showed that the Hough Transform can be subdivided into several constrained subproblems [17]. He proposed a new HT, called the *constrained hough transform* (CnsHT), where each of these subproblems examines a subset of the parameter space by considering only those pixel sets that include pixels of defined properties. This decomposition allows for propagation of the localization error of the edge features into the parameter space and for randomization used for limiting the number of subproblems that need to be examined.

A *non-probabilistic* method inspired by the probabilistic algorithms is the *modified hough transform* (MHT) [18]. The MHT uses a many-to-one mapping, but there is no randomization during the accumulation. From an ordered group of all edge points, a seed point is selected according to the sequence of the elements in the set. The seed point is processed with all of the remaining points from the set. For all pairs, parameters corresponding to the line passing through this couple are calculated. The seed point allows to use only a 1D θ-histogram as an accumulator. After the accumulation of all pairs with the same seed point, peaks are detected in the parameter space. The maxima are saved in another space and edge points corresponding to the detected lines are removed. The seed point is also removed from the set and the algorithm is reinitialized with the next seed point from the sequence.

A weighted accumulation using Bayesian updating scheme was presented in the work *error propagation for the hough transform* (EPHT) by Ji and Haralick [19]. The algorithm starts with a θ estimation from the gradient measurements and computes ϱ from the estimated θ and from the edge point. It is assumed that the input image is corrupted with a noise which results to uncertainty of the estimated line parameters. The contribution of the edge point to the parameter space therefore depends on the uncertainty associated with the estimated parameters with perturbation.

Determination of a dominant distribution in the parameter space is the essence of the *hough transform with principal axis analysis* (PAAHT) [20]. The dominant distribution is determined using a θ-histogram. The elements of the θ-histogram are sorted according to the occurrences in the histogram. The first peak then represents the first principal axis in the image space and the remaining peaks are ranked accordingly. The searching priority for peak detection in the parameter space is set according to the angle of the principal axis. When all possible line segments in this angle have been extracted, the histogram count at this angle is reset to avoid being detected again and this process is done iteratively until all line segments are extracted for all angles.

The SHT is limited in accuracy by the voting nature; however, Shapiro considers a non-voting alternative called *hough-green transform* (HGT) [21]. The HGT is based on tracing object contours ("trace" here means a sequence of adjacent boundary pixels to be acquired), because processing the contours enable shape analysis without any loss of information. The goal of the HGT is to derive the HT space, i.e., the set of mappings from the contour trace. The implementation is based on angular projections. The whole recursive process contains the following steps: contour tracing, vertical projection evaluation, rotating the trace samples, and ϱ-resampling if required.

For sparse and long lines, a special algorithm called the *gridding hough transform* (GrHT) [22] is suitable. The input image is overlaid by a grid which divides it into subblocks. It is assumed that a long straight line intersects a block in two points. For each subblock, its boundaries are searched for edge points. Once a couple of edge points is found, a linelet candidate connecting these points is considered. The number of edge points inside the subblock which lie on the linelet is used for evaluation. After processing this procedure for all subblocks, a set of linelets is obtained. Each element from the set votes for a unique couple of (θ, ρ) parameters in the Hough space.

When a bins exceeds a given threshold, its parameters define a line candidate which is finally checked whether it is a real line.

Song and Lyu proposed a method utilizing the image space to help accelerate the whole process and detect the line thickness—the *line thickness hough transform* (THT) [23]. This method is suitable mainly for large-size images, for example engineering drawings. Similar to the SHT there are three major steps: HT accumulation, peak selection and sorting, and line verification. These steps are modified in the following manner. In the voting step, only a small portion of pixels–called feature points— participate in the voting. The feature points are medial points of line-like areas obtained by orthogonal run-length scanning of the input image. For each feature point, a gradient prediction is performed using the lengths of diagonal and perpendicular runs passing the feature point. The lengths also determine the weight for the vote to favor thick lines. After voting, the parameter space is searched for local peaks over a given threshold and sorted in a descending order to start a process of verification of the line segments, searching for the strongest one.

Improvement of line segments detection by expansion of the Hough space by a third parameter was presented by Cha et al. [24]. The *extended hough transform* (EHT) uses two dual 2D Hough spaces based on the *slope-intercept* parameterization augmented by a third parameter—the horizontal or vertical coordinate within the image space. This extension allows for more accurate detection of short line segments, which can be missed in the standard HT variants.

The problem of finding the location and orientation of straight lines as an inverse problem is discussed by Aggarwal and Karl [25]. Their *regularized hough transform* (RegHT) is based on the use of the inverse Radon operator, which relates to the parameters of the detected line. The algorithm repeatedly calculates the Radon transforms and back-projections using regularizers. Through the choice of the regularizer, it is possible to suppress noisy regions in the Hough space which arise due to noise and nonlinear features and at the same time to preserve features which correspond to lines in the input image.

Most of the HT modifications have the parameter space built by uniformly quantizing the θ and ϱ ranges. Duan et al. [26] showed that a non-uniform Hough space is more adequate to discriminate the straightlines in a digitized image, because these two parameters are dependent on line angles and line segment lengths. The key of *nonuniform hough transform* (NUHT) is that θ is nonuniformly sampled and the quantization interval of ϱ is different for different values of θ.

Clustering of approximately collinear feature pixels is the first step of the *hough transform with improved voting scheme* (IVHT) [27]. For each cluster, an elliptical kernel is computed considering its line fitting uncertainty. Before voting of the kernel in the parameter space, a culling strategy is used to avoid casting votes for kernels whose contributions are negligible. Finally, after voting of all kernels, the resulting parameter space is smoothed and searched for peaks.

Using all pixels of the image (i.e. as much information as available) and a statistical kernel modeling to generalize the Hough transform is the main idea of the *statistical hough transform* (StHT) [28]. The result of the StHT is a density function which encodes the local appearance-based measures. Since it is considering all pixels, the StHT is more computationally expensive then the SHT.

Because HT is very often used for the detection of objects in real-world images, the input set of the edge pixels can include many noisy pixels from, for example, textures such as grass, bricks, etc. Such textures cause false peaks in the Hough space and thus produce false positives in the final results. Gua et al. introduced a voting scheme utilizing *surround suppression* (SSHT) [29]. By giving small weights to edges in the textured regions and large weights to edges on strong and clear boundaries, the surround suppression improves the accuracy of line detection on real-world images. On the other hand, this approach is slower compared to the SHT.

3.2 Probabilistic Methods

The *probabilistic* Hough Transforms share a common feature: random picking of a subset of the edge points from the set of all edges detected in the input image. Such subsampling of the input edges allows for a significant computational saving since only a small subset of points are considered (accumulated). Many methods from this group use many-to-one mapping, i.e., instead of a hyperplane in the parameter space, only one point has to be accumulated. That is why a sparse structure (e.g., a linked list), instead of the nD uniform accumulator space, is sometimes used. In this section, the *randomized hough transform* and its modifications is presented first, followed by the rest of the methods in the chronological order.

The basic RHT by Xu et al. [4] is suitable for detection of curves expressed by n parameters (i.e. with n degrees of freedom). In the algorithm, n pixels, which uniquely define a curve, are randomly selected and mapped to the corresponding point in the parameter space. In the case of line detection it means that pairs of points are selected and accumulated until a number of votes for one line is over a given threshold. When such a maximum is reached, the parameters of the curve (line) are derived, edge points coincident with the curve are removed, and the algorithm runs again with the remaining pixels. Some implementations of the RHT for line detection use the point distance criterion, where selected pairs of pixels must not be too far or too near from each other; such a limitation guarantees higher probability that the pixels lie on a common line and that their contribution to the accumulator space will be meaningful.

The windowing versions of the RHT, called *windowed RHT* (WRHT) and *random windowed* RHT (RWRHT) were presented by Kälviäinen et al. [30]. Both of them use random sampling, many-to-one mapping and local information around an edge point. In the RWRHT, a window location is randomly selected from the binary edge image. The window size $m \times m$ is also randomized. This window sampling is repeated for R times (R could be a function of m) or until a predefined threshold is reached. Lines are detected one by one and after a new line is detected, its pixels are removed from the set of the edges. The WRHT is a simpler version that selects one edge point randomly, fits a curve to pixels in its $m \times m$ neighborhood, evaluates the fitting error, and if the error is less than a given threshold, the corresponding cell is increased (vote accumulated).

The RWRHT is a part of another *probabilistic* HT which uses the mean shift clustering for finding maxima in the Hough space. The *mean shift hough transform* (MSHT) [31] uses the RWRHT- based approach to update an accurate Hough space and then the accumulator is clustered by the variable bandwidth mean shift algorithm. Thus, the clustering process allows for using accurate Hough parameters and the algorithm is capable of detecting a single line even when the pixels along the line are not exactly collinear.

An extension of the RHT, called the *connective RHT* (CRHT) [32] better utilizes local information than the original RHT. In the CRHT, a $w \times w$ window is first randomly picked with an edge point in the center. In the next step, only points connected with the middle point by an 8-path are used. The CRHT fits a curve to these points, for example, by the least squares method. If the fitting error is within a tolerance, parameters of the curve are mapped into the Hough space. Like the basic RHT, after reaching a required number of votes, the curve can be removed and the algorithm reruns.

An iterative process of two RHTs was introduced as the *dynamic RHT* (DRHT) [33]. First, the original RHT is run until the voting threshold is reached by one of the cells. Points near to the detected line are used in the second RHT iteration. The accumulator resolution and the threshold are usually selected to be higher in the second stage. Because the number of sampled points in the second step is relatively small and both the resolution and the threshold are low in the first step, the computational time can be significantly spared.

An extension to the three-point RHT and a generalization to N-point RHT was proposed by Mochizuky et al. as the *N-point hough transform* (NPHT) [34]. The third point is used to avoid the selection of meaningless first and second sample points, which are used for the computation of the parameters of a line. This additional sample point guarantees the accuracy and robustness. The N-point Hough transform evaluates the accuracy and robustness of a computed line using additional $N - 2$ points for each line. The NPHT algorithm uses a back-voting process, when the additional points are searched on the line defined by the first pair of points.

The probabilistic approach can also be applied to the *dynamic combinatorial hough transform* (DCHT) presented by Ben-Tzvi et al. [11]. In the DCHT, the θ–ϱ line parameterization is used. All two-point combinations with the seed point, which can be selected randomly, are accumulated into a single value in a θ-histogram. Again, after reaching a predefined threshold in the 1D histogram, the detected line is removed and the sampling procedure continues until all points have been removed. If the threshold is not reached, the seed point is removed and another one is used for the sampling procedure.

A method different from the RHT in both the randomization and accumulation is the *probabilistic hough transform* by Kyriaty et al. (ProbHT) [5]. As with SHT, a one-to-many mapping from the image space to the parameter space is used. Contrary to the SHT, rather than using all edge points for accumulation, only a small, randomly selected subset is used. The smaller the cardinality of the subset, the faster the algorithm is, but fewer features can be detected.

Sometimes it is advantageous to choose subsets of edge points of an arbitrary size randomly. The method presented as the *monte-carlo hough transform* (MCHT) [35] is based on this idea. For line detection it means to randomly pick one or two edge points and accumulate the evidence for the corresponding line, or for the single point. For circles, the set has one, two, or three points. Because the number of increments in the accumulation space is smaller than in the case of the SHT, the algorithm is much faster.

An algorithm very similar to the DCHT is the *connective hough transform* (ConHT) [36]. The similarity is in the random selection of the seed point and in the use of a 1D θ-accumulator. The difference is in the accumulation, which is in the case of the ConHT performed row by row (referred to as *ordered accumulation*) in order to have connectivity between the accumulator points. The lines which are more vertical than horizontal require their own accumulator. Thus, for ConHT, two accumulator arrays are needed.

A modification of the ProbHT, named the *progressive probabilistic hough transform* (PPHT) [37], was proposed by Galambos et al. The PPHT minimizes the amount of computation needed to detect lines by exploiting the difference in the fraction of votes needed to reliably detect lines with different numbers of supporting points. The algorithm randomly selects edge pixels from a pixel set and updates the accumulator. If a bin in the accumulator reaches a given threshold, a corresponding corridor in the input image, defined by the parameters associated with the bin, is searched for the longest segment. The pixels of the segment are removed from the set, unvoted from the accumulator and if the line segment is longer than the minimum length, it is added to the output list. The algorithm tends to find salient features first, what is a property suited for real-time applications with a fixed processing time frame. An extension of this method [38] is using gradient information to control the voting process and to assign pixels correctly to a line in order to enhance both the accuracy and the performance of the PPHT.

The conventional Hough transforms transform the image points into representations of lines in the parameter space. Since a line segment in the image actually has a non-zero width, Ching et al. propose to transfer an image point into a belt of accumulators [39]. In the *hough transform using belts* (BHT), the width of a belt is a function of the width of the line segment in the image. The reason why this method belongs to *probabilistic* HTs is in random selection of a subset from the set of all edge points on a line segment for the segment approximation. If there is more than one line in the image, the algorithm is applied iteratively with removing the edge pixels with a small distance from the detected line segment.

A framework in which different *probabilistic* Hough Transforms can be understood was provided by Walsh as the *importance sampling hough transform* (ISHT) [40]. The algorithm uses two distributions: an importance sampling distribution and a target distribution. The target distribution measures the fitness of the curve given by parameter θ to the edge point. After taking a set of random parameters θ from the sampling distribution, for each sample, the importance weight is calculated.

The weight depends on the target distribution. Detection of peaks runs on the weighted sample of parameters and for each found line, the corresponding points are removed from the next processing. As the stopping condition, for example, the total number of parameter samples can be used.

An RHT modification aimed to improve both the robustness and the accuracy by analytically propagating the errors associated with image pixels to the estimated curve parameters was proposed by Li and Xie [41]. The algorithm of the randomized *hough transform with error propagation* (EPRHT) first selects a seed point that is most likely located on the curve. Then, other pixels are picked to calculate the parameters of the line that passes through the pair. For updating the accumulator space, a voting kernel that is a smooth function of the differences in the parameter values is used. This approach allows to quantitatively determine the contribution of feature points to the curve parameters and to statistically select the seed pixels that most likely are located on the curves and that produce the best curve estimation.

The *hough transform with eliminating particle swarm optimization* (EPSOHT) [42] is one of the newest HT modifications which focuses on reduction of computational time and improving the performance. In this method, the solution parameters after transformation are considered as the particle positions, and the eliminating particle swarm optimization (EPSO) algorithm searches the optimal solution by eliminating the weakest particles to speed up the computation. The accumulator space is utilized as a fitness function of the EPSO algorithm.

A method which exhibits some similarities with the MHT and *windowed RHT* (described above) is the *improved hough transform* (IHT) by Duan et al. [43]. This algorithm sequentially scans for a feature point P from the binary edge image, and picks it out as the seed point. Then, a $m \times m$ window centered at P is selected and searched for the connected pixels. For all feature points in the window, the parameters of lines passing through point P and the respective feature point are calculated. These parameters vote in the accumulator space specific for the window. The space is searched for maxima and when the search is successful, the weighted mean value of the parameters which voted for this cell is calculated. If the maximum is over a given threshold, the calculation is extended to the whole image, where a sufficient number of edge points supporting the line are searched. Lines with enough votes are sent to the output and point P is deleted. The algorithm continues until all the feature points are eliminated from the image.

3.3 HT Variants Using Special Hardware

The Hough transform algorithm consists of simple operations (accumulation: two multiplications ane one addition; peak detection: max). However, these operations are repeated many times—depending on the input set dimension and the resolution of the accumulator space. The computational time increases exponentially with the dimension of the parameter space and linearly with the number of the accumulated edge points. Fortunately, the algorithm can be easily parallelized, since different subimages of the input image can be processed separately.

All mentioned hardware implementations use the $\theta-\varrho$ parameterization, as it is the de-facto standard. Only recently, Bailey [44] compared the $\theta-\varrho$, slope-intercept and the parallel coordinates (Chap. 4) based parameterizations. He found and showed on experiments that the linear parameterizations are suitable for hardware implementation and superior to the $\theta-\varrho$ parameterization.

Contrary to the software implementations, the hardware-centered ones use various ways for calculation of the goniometric functions. The software implementations use lookup-tables almost exclusively. In the hardware implementations, the LUTs are rare. Implementing the LUT would require the circuitry that is not necessary when other methods are used, but the software implementations running on general purpose processors implement LUTs virtually at no cost.

The hardware used for implementing the Hough transform-based line detection nicely illustrated the advances in (programmable) hardware design over time. The implementations used application-specific circuits first, but soon moved to programmable hardware. The latest implementations use modern complex FPGAs that can be reprogrammed frequently and even during the processing.

Hanahara et al. [45] designed a real-time processor for line detection using TTL circuits and a MC68000 processor. Instead of a massively parallel approach, the hardware design is serial in its nature. The calculation of ϱ and the parameter space accumulation are pipelined. The whole line detection process takes 0.79 s for an image with 1,024 feature points (edges) and 8-bit 512×512 parameter space.

Rhodes et al. [46] used a generic restructurable VLSI chip (RVLSI) to implement line detection based on the Hough transform. The chip consists of many multiply-add blocks with an interconnection matrix that can be once configured by laser cutting/soldering. The functional blocks can be tested after fabrication, so that even some chips with small defects can be used. The resulting processor ran at real-time frame rates, i.e., roughly 20ms per frame.

Fisher et al. [47] implemented Hough transform on a device called scan line array processor (SLAP) which they designed for high-performance and low-cost image processing. The device consists of processing elements arranged in a linear array. Each processing element is a SIMD vector processor and it processes a single column of the input image so that the element array scans the input image row by row. The accumulator array is distributed between the processing elements and each accumulator cell is separate. The cells are moved between the processing elements so that the proper cell is connected to the element that processes edges of the corresponding line. The movement of a given cell does not depend on the image data directly; it depends only on the edge's θ and ϱ.

Nakanishi and Ogura [48] used content-addressable memory (CAM) to implement the Hough transform. The CAM can perform extremely simple operations in a massively parallel way. For example, integer addition takes roughly 40 clock cycles, but it can be performed on all selected words in the memory at once. Both the voting process and the search for local maxima were implemented using the CAM.

With a single CAM chip, real-time detection was possible for images 256×256 pixels and two CAM chips allowed real-time processing of images 512×512 pixels.

Tagzout et al. [49] improved the *incremental hough transform* to fit the field programmable gate arrays (FPGA). The incremental Hough transform approximates the sine curve in the $\theta-\varrho$ parameterization by linear segments. After several steps, full calculation is performed in order to reset the accumulated error. Tagzout improved the IHT by an incremental modification of the slope of the line segments so the full calculation is required less often. The discretized curve in the $\theta-\varrho$ space is

$$\varrho_n = x \cos(n\varepsilon) + y \sin(n\varepsilon). \tag{3.1}$$

The IHT is described by recurrent equations

$$\varrho_{n+1} = \varrho_n + \varepsilon\varrho'_n, \tag{3.2}$$

$$\varrho'_{n+1} = \varrho'_n + \varepsilon\varrho_n, \tag{3.3}$$

$$\varrho_0 = x, \tag{3.4}$$

$$\varrho'_0 = y. \tag{3.5}$$

With the size of the parameter space being 2^n, the improved IHT consists mostly of additions and shifts; thus it minimizes the requirements on the hardware resources.

Maharatna and Banerjee [50] proposed an asynchronous architecture for Hough transform that uses CORDIC (Coordinate Rotation Digital Computer). The CORDIC is an iterative process for computation of vector rotations and it is frequently used to calculate trigonometric functions. Any matrix rotation can be split to a series of "smaller" rotations

$$\mathbf{x}' = R\mathbf{x} = R_n \cdots R_1\mathbf{x}. \tag{3.6}$$

The smaller rotations can be performed in both directions, not only in the direction of R. For the "classical" calculation of goniometric functions, a set of basic rotations is tabulated. For the Hough transform, it is beneficial to split the rotation to very small steps. For small values, $\sin(x) \equiv x$ and for the curve rasterization, small steps are required anyway. By small incremental rotations, the whole voting curve is calculated and accumulated in parallel or in a pipelined manner.

Chern and Lu [51] used their array processor architecture to implement the Hough transform. Their architecture consists of an array of simple processors that process one column (i.e. one θ value) of the parameter space each. Each processor has some amount of memory to store the parameter space and a separate incrementation block. The number of processors limits the number of line angles which the system detects in one pass.

Karabernou and Terranti [52] combined the CORDIC- based HW implementation of the Hough transform with the restriction of the rasterized curve to a segment of the parameter space based on the edge gradient detected by the Sobel operator. The implementation was done using FPGA. They implemented the CORDIC algorithm in the iterative way in order to limit the amount of required hardware resources.

Although the iterative implementation is significantly slower than the parallel one, the resulting system was capable of real-time processing of many common video resolutions with the exception of the HD ones.

Jolly and Fleury [53] improved the CORDIC-based HT by splitting the parameter space into blocks. The blocks can be processed in parallel. More importantly, based on the line angle intervals, the circuitry can be simplified. Each block requires less tabulated microrotations and the implementation is also more precise in the result. The implementation also uses two-port BRAMs, common on FPGAs, to speed up the read-increment-write part of the accumulation process.

Satzoda et al. [54] have proven the additive property of the $\theta-\varrho$ parameterization. A curve $\varrho_O(A, \theta)$ is the sinusoidal curve for a point A with respect to the origin O. The curve can be split to

$$\varrho_O(A, \theta) = \varrho_O(B, \theta) + \varrho_B(A, \theta), \tag{3.7}$$

so that the point A can be expressed with respect to another origin. This allows to split the image space to a grid and compute the sinusoidal curves only locally in every block. These blocks can be processed independently on the local Hough space and then merged together to form the global Hough space. The "offset" curves can be precomputed, because they are known in advance.

Suchitra et al. [55] reduced the required number of iterations for the CORDIC algorithm by using a binary tree. Instead of using linear addition, the angles are added and subtracted during a tree traversal. Therefore, only eight iterations are necessary to achieve a precision better than one angular degree.

References

1. Kälviäinen, H., Hirvonen, P., Xu, L., Oja, E.: Comparisons of probabilistic and non-probabilistic hough transforms. In: Proceedings of 3rd European Conference on Computer Vision ECCV'94, pp. 351–360 (1994)
2. Hough, P.V.C.: Method and means for recognizing complex patterns. US Patent 3,069,654 (1962)
3. Duda, R.O., Hart, P.E.: Use of the Hough transformation to detect lines and curves in pictures. Commun. ACM **15**(1), 11–15 (1972). DOI http://doi.acm.org/10.1145/361237.361242
4. Xu, L., Oja, E., Kultanen, P.: A new curve detection method: Randomized Hough Transform (RHT). Pattern Recognit. Lett. **11**, 331–338 (1990). doi:10.1016/0167-8655(90)90042-Z
5. Kiryati, N., Eldar, Y., Bruckstein, A.M.: A probabilistic hough transform. Pattern Recogn. **24**(4), 303–316 (1991). DOI http://dx.doi.org/10.1016/0031-3203(91)90073-E
6. Li, H., Lavin, M.A., Le Master, R.J.: Fast hough transform: A hierarchical approach. Comput. Vision Graph. Image Process. **36**, 139–161 (1986). DOI http://dx.doi.org/10.1016/0734-189X(86)90073-3
7. Illingworth, J., Kittler, J.: The adaptive hough transform. IEEE Trans. Pattern Anal. Mach. Intell. **9**(5), 690–698 (1987). DOI http://dx.doi.org/10.1109/TPAMI.1987.4767964
8. Niblack, W., Petkovic, D.: On improving the accuracy of the hough transform: theory, simulations, and experiments. In: Proceedings of the Computer Society Conference on Computer

Vision and Pattern Recognition CVPR '88., pp. 574–579 (1988). DOI10.1109/CVPR.1988.
196293

9. Kiryati, N., Bruckstein, A.: Antialiasing the hough transform. CVGIP: Graphical Models
   Imag. Process. **53**(3), 213–222 (1991). DOI10.1016/1049-9652(91)90043-J. http://www.
   sciencedirect.com/science/article/pii/104996529190043J

10. Princen, J., Illingworth, J., Kittler, J.: A hierarchical approach to line extraction. In: Proceed-
    ings of the IEEE Computer Society Conference on Computer Vision and Pattern Recognition
    CVPR '89., pp. 92–97 (1989). DOI10.1109/CVPR.1989.37833

11. Ben-Tzvi, D., Sandler, M.: A combinatorial hough transform. Pattern Recognit. Lett.
    11(3), 167–174 (1990). DOI10.1016/0167-8655(90)90002-J. http://www.sciencedirect.com/
    science/article/pii/016786559090002J

12. Liang, P.: A new transform for curve detection. In: Proceedings of the Third International
    Conference on Computer Vision 1990, pp. 748–751 (1990). DOI 10.1109/ICCV.1990.139633.

13. Stephens, R.: Probabilistic approach to the hough transform. Image Vis. Comput. **9**(1), 66–71
    (1991). DOI10.1016/0262-8856(91)90051-P. http://www.sciencedirect.com/science/article/
    pii/026288569190051P. The first BMVC 1990

14. Atiquzzaman, M.: Multiresolution hough transform-an efficient method of detecting patterns
    in images. IEEE Trans. Pattern Anal. Mach. Intell. **14**(11), 1090–1095 (1992). DOI10.1109/
    34.166623. http://dx.doi.org/10.1109/34.166623

15. Ser, P.K., Siu, W.C.: Sampling hough algorithm for the detection of lines and curves. In:
    Proceedings of the IEEE International Symposium on Circuits and Systems ISCAS '92,
    vol. 5, pp. 2497–2500 (1992). DOI10.1109/ISCAS.1992.230479

16. Palmer, P., Petrou, M., Kittler, J.: A hough transform algorithm with a 2d hypothesis testing
    kernel. CVGIP: Image Underst. **58**(2), 221–234 (1993). DOI10.1006/ciun.1993.1039. http://
    www.sciencedirect.com/science/article/pii/S1049966083710399

17. Olson, C.F.: Constrained hough transforms for curve detection. Comput. Vis. Image Underst.
    73(3), 329–345 (1999). DOI10.1006/cviu.1998.0728. http://www.sciencedirect.com/science/
    article/pii/S1077314298907287

18. Chutatape, O., Guo, L.: A modified hough transform for line detection and its performance.
    Pattern Recognit. **32**(2), 181–192 (1999). DOI10.1016/S0031-3203(98)00140-X. http://www.
    sciencedirect.com/science/article/pii/S003132039800140X

19. Ji, Q., Haralick, R.M.: Error propagation for the hough transform. Pattern Recogn. Lett. **22**(6–7),
    813–823 (2001). DOI10.1016/S0167-8655(01)00026-5. http://dx.doi.org/10.1016/S0167-
    8655(01)00026-5

20. Rau, J.Y., Chen, L.C.: Fast straight lines detection using hough transform with principal axis
    analysis. J. Photogrammetry Remote Sens. **8**, 15–34 (2003)

21. Shapiro, V.: Fast and precise angular projection evaluation (hough-green transform). In. Pro-
    ceedings of SPIE 5300 (2004)

22. Yu, X., Lai, H., Liu, S., Leong, H.: A gridding hough transform for detecting the straight lines
    in sports video. In: IEEE International Conference on Multimedia and Expo ICME 2005, p. 4
    (2005). DOI10.1109/ICME.2005.1521474

23. Song, J., Lyu, M.R.: A hough transform based line recognition method utilizing both parameter
    space and image space. Pattern Recogn. **38**(4), 539–552 (2005). DOI10.1016/j.patcog.2004.
    09.003. http://dx.doi.org/10.1016/j.patcog.2004.09.003

24. Cha, J., Cofer, R., Kozaitis, S.: Extended hough transform for linear feature detection.
    Pattern Recognit. **39**(6), 1034–1043 (2006). DOI10.1016/j.patcog.2005.05.014. http://www.
    sciencedirect.com/science/article/pii/S0031320305002335

25. Aggarwal, N., Karl, W.: Line detection in images through regularized hough transform. IEEE
    Trans. Image Process. **15**(3), 582–591 (2006). doi:10.1109/TIP.2005.863021

26. Duan, H., Liu, X., Liu, H.: A nonuniform quantization of hough space for the detection of
    straight line segments. In: 2nd International Conference on Pervasive Computing and Appli-
    cations, ICPCA 2007, pp. 149–153 (2007). DOI10.1109/ICPCA.2007.4365429

27. Fernandes, L.A., Oliveira, M.M.: Real-time line detection through an improved hough trans-
    form voting scheme. Pattern Recognit. **41**(1), 299–314 (2008). DOI10.1016/j.patcog.2007.04.
    003. http://www.sciencedirect.com/science/article/pii/S0031320307001823

28. Dahyot, R.: Statistical hough transform. IEEE Transactions on Pattern Analysis and Machine Intelligence 31, 1502–1509 (2009). DOI http://doi.ieeecomputersociety.org/10.1109/TPAMI.2008.288

29. Guo, S., Pridmore, T., Kong, Y., Zhang, X.: An improved hough transform voting scheme utilizing surround suppression. Pattern Recognit. Lett. **30**(13), 1241–1252 (2009). DOI10.1016/j.patrec.2009.05.003. http://www.sciencedirect.com/science/article/pii/S0167865509001032

30. Kälviäinen, H., Xu, L.E.O.: Recent versions of the hough transform and the randomized hough transform: Overview and comparisons. Technical Report, Lappeenranta University of Technology, Finland (1993)

31. Bandera, A., Pérez-Lorenzo, J.M., Bandera, J.P., Sandoval, F.: Mean shift based clustering of hough domain for fast line segment detection. Pattern Recogn. Lett. **27**(6), 578–586 (2006). DOI10.1016/j.patrec.2005.09.023. http://dx.doi.org/10.1016/j.patrec.2005.09.023

32. Kälviäinen, H., Hirvonen, P.: Connective randomized hough transform (crht). In: Proceedings of the 9th Scandinavian Conference on Image Analysis, pp. 1029–1036 (1995)

33. Kälviäinen, H., Hirvonen, P., Xu, L., Oja, E.: Probabilistic and non-probabilistic hough transforms: overview and comparisons. Image Vis. Comput. **13**(4), 239–252 (1995). DOI10.1016/0262-8856(95)99713-B. http://www.sciencedirect.com/science/article/pii/026288569599713B

34. Mochizuki, Y., Torii, A., Imiya, A.: N-point hough transform for line detection. J. Vis. Comun. Image Represent. **20**, 242–253 (2009). doi:10.1016/j.jvcir.2009.01.004

35. Shvaytser, H., Bergen, J.: Monte carlo hough transforms. In: Proceedings of the 7th Scandinavian Conference on Image and Analysis (1991)

36. Yuen, S.Y.K., Lam, T.S.L., Leung, N.K.D.: Connective hough transform. Image Vis. Comput. **11**(5), 295–301 (1993). DOI10.1016/0262-8856(93)90007-4. http://www.sciencedirect.com/science/article/pii/0262885693900074

37. Galambos, C., Matas, J., Kittler, J.: Progressive probabilistic hough transform for line detection. In: IEEE Computer Society Conference on Computer Vision and Pattern Recognition, vol. 1, pp. 2 vol. (xxiii+637+663) (1999). DOI10.1109/CVPR.1999.786993

38. Galambos, C., Kittler, J., Matas, J.: Using gradient information to enhance the progressive probabilistic hough transform. In: Proceedings of the 15th International Conference on Pattern Recognition , vol. 3, pp. 560–563 (2000). DOI10.1109/ICPR.2000.903607

39. Ching, Y.T.: Detecting line segments in an image –a new implementation for hough transform. Pattern Recognit. Lett. **22**(3–4), 421–429 (2001). DOI10.1016/S0167-8655(00)00130-6. http://www.sciencedirect.com/science/article/pii/S0167865500001306

40. Walsh, D., Raftery, A.E.: Accurate and efficient curve detection in images: the importance sampling hough transform. Pattern Recognit. **35**(7), 1421–1431 (2002). DOI10.1016/S0031-3203(01)00114-5. http://www.sciencedirect.com/science/article/pii/S0031320301001145

41. Li, Q., Xie, Y.: Randomised hough transform with error propagation for line and circle detection. Pattern Anal. Appl. 55–64 (2003)

42. Cheng, H.D., Guo, Y., Zhang, Y.: A novel hough transform based on eliminating particle swarm optimization and its applications. Pattern Recogn. **42**, 1959–1969 (2009). doi:10.1016/j.patcog.2008.11.028

43. Duan, D., Xie, M., Mo, Q., Han, Z., Wan, Y.: An improved hough transform for line detection. In: International Conference on Computer Application and System Modeling (ICCASM), vol. 2, pp. V2–354 -V2-357 (2010). DOI10.1109/ICCASM.2010.5620827

44. Bailey, D.G.: Considerations for hardware hough transforms. In: Image and Vision Computing, New Zealand, Australia (2011)

45. Hanahara, K., Maruyama, T., Uchiyama, T.: A real-time processor for the hough transform. IEEE Trans. Pattern Anal. Mach. Intell. **10**(1), 121–125 (1988). DOI10.1109/34.3876. http://dx.doi.org/10.1109/34.3876

46. Rhodes, F.M., Dituri, J.J., Chapman, G.H., Emerson, B.E., Soares, A.M.: A monolithic hough transform processor based on restructurable vlsi. IEEE Trans. Pattern Anal. Mach. Intell. **10**(1), 106–110 (1988). DOI10.1109/34.3873. http://dx.doi.org/10.1109/34.3873

47. Fisher, A., Highnam, P.: Computing the hough transform on a scan line array processor. IEEE Trans. Pattern Anal. Mach. Intell. **11**(3), 262–265 (1989). doi:10.1109/34.21795
48. Nakanishi, M., Ogura, T.: A real-time cam-based hough transform algorithm and its performance evaluation. In: Proceedings of the 13th International Conference on Pattern Recognition, vol. 2, pp. 516–521 (1996). DOI10.1109/ICPR.1996.546878
49. Tagzout, S., Achour, K., Djekoune, O.: Hough transform algorithm for fpga implementation. In: IEEE Workshop on Signal Processing Systems, SiPS 2000, pp. 384–393 (2000). DOI10.1109/SIPS.2000.886737
50. Maharatna, K., Banerjee, S.: A vlsi array architecture for hough transform. Pattern Recognit. **34**(7), 1503–1512 (2001). DOI10.1016/S0031-3203(00)00080-7. http://www.sciencedirect.com/science/article/pii/S0031320300000807
51. Chern, M.Y., Lu, Y.H.: Design and integration of parallel hough-transform chips for high-speed line detection. In: Proceedings of the 11th International Conference on Parallel and Distributed Systems, vol. 2, pp. 42–46 (2005). DOI10.1109/ICPADS.2005.126
52. Karabernou, S.M., Terranti, F.: Real-time fpga implementation of hough transform using gradient and cordic algorithm. Image Vis. Comput. **23**(11), 1009–1017 (2005). DOI10.1016/j.imavis.2005.07.004. http://dx.doi.org/10.1016/j.imavis.2005.07.004
53. Jolly, E., Fleury, M.: Multi-sector algorithm for hardware acceleration of the general hough transform. Image Vis. Comput. **24**(9), 970–976 (2006). DOI10.1016/j.imavis.2006.02.016. http://www.sciencedirect.com/science/article/pii/S0262885606000989
54. Satzoda, R., Suchitra, S., Srikanthan, T.: Parallelizing the hough transform computation. IEEE Signal Process. Lett. **15**, 297–300 (2008). doi:10.1109/LSP.2008.917804
55. Suchitra, S., Satzoda, R., Srikanthan, T.: Accelerating cordic for hough transform. In: Proceedings of the 12th International Symposium on Integrated Circuits, ISIC '09, pp. 167–170 (2009)

Chapter 4
PClines: Line Parameterization Based on Parallel Coordinates

Recently, parallel coordinates [1] were used for parameterizing lines for the Hough transform [2, 3]. This parameterization, referred to as the Parallel-Axis Transform (PAT) or PClines, is a point-to-line mapping. This chapter introduces the parameterization in detail. First, Sect. 4.1 reviews the basic information about the parallel coordinates needed for understanding the parameterization. Then, the parameterization is introduced in Sect. 4.2, and a brief analysis of its accuracy is given in Sect. 4.3.

4.1 Parallel Coordinates

A common way to visualize vectors in N-dimensional Euclidean space is by using Cartesian coordinates, where each vector in a given N-dimensional vector space is represented by exactly one point in the N-dimensional coordinate system. However, visualization of spaces with more than two dimensions on two-dimensional drawing equipment (paper, computer monitor, etc.) is only possible by projection, which, especially for higher dimensionalities, might not be intuitive and can severely restrict the amount of information presented at a time.

The parallel coordinate system [1] represents the vector space by axes which are mutually parallel. Each N-dimensional vector is then represented by $N - 1$ lines connecting the axes—see Fig. 4.1. In this text, we will be using a Euclidean plane with a $u - v$ Cartesian coordinate system to define positions of points in the space of parallel coordinates. For defining these points, a notation $(u, v, w)_{\mathbb{P}^2}$ will be used for homogeneous coordinates in the projective space $\mathbb{P}^2$ and $(u, v)_{\mathbb{E}^2}$ will be used for Cartesian coordinates in the Euclidean space $\mathbb{E}^2$.

In the two-dimensional case, points in the $x - y$ space are represented as lines in the space of parallel coordinates. Representations of collinear points intersect at one point—the representation of a line (see Fig. 4.2). Based on this relation, it is possible to define a point-to-line mapping between these spaces. For some cases, such as line $\ell : y = x$, the corresponding point $\overline{\ell}$ lies in infinity (it is an ideal point). Projective

A. Herout et al., *Real-Time Detection of Lines and Grids*,
SpringerBriefs in Computer Science, DOI: 10.1007/978-1-4471-4414-4_4,

Fig. 4.1 Representation of a 5-dimensional vector in parallel coordinates. The vector is represented by its coordinates $C_1, \ldots, C_5$ on axes $x'_1, \ldots, x'_5$, connected by a complete polyline (composed of four *infinite lines*)

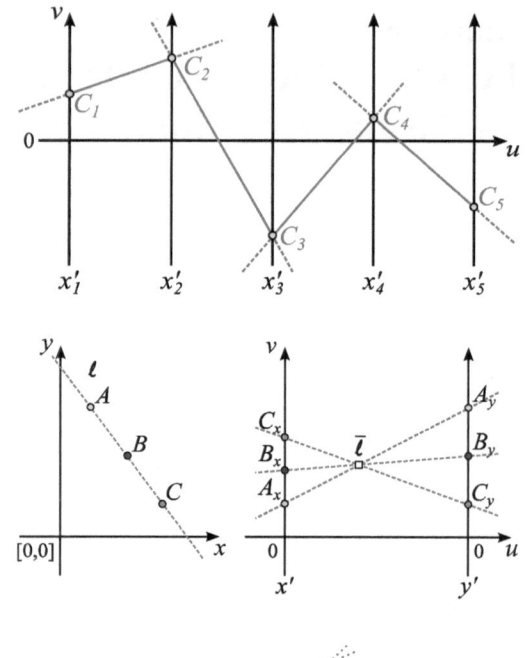

Fig. 4.2 Three collinear points in parallel coordinates: (*left*) Cartesian space, (*right*) space of parallel coordinates. Line ℓ is represented by point $\bar{\ell}$ in parallel coordinates

Fig. 4.3 Points $\bar{\ell}_{i,i+1}$ exactly define a set of four equations which determine a line in a 5-dimensional space

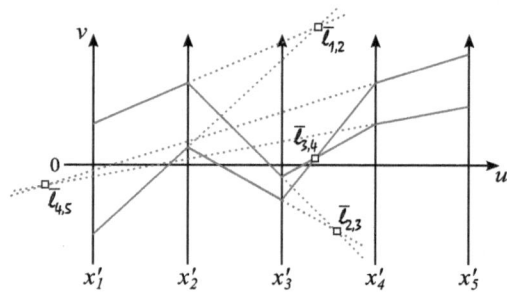

space $\mathbb{P}^2$ (contrary to the Euclidean $\mathbb{E}^2$ space) provides coordinates for these special cases. A relation between line $\ell : ax + by + c = 0$ (denoted as $[a, b, c]$) and its representing point $\bar{\ell}$ can be defined by mapping:

$$\ell : [a, b, c] \rightarrow \bar{\ell} : (db, -c, a + b)_{\mathbb{P}^2}, \qquad (4.1)$$

where d is the distance between parallel axes x' and y'.

This can be generalized for higher dimensions since a line in $\mathbb{E}^N$ is a set of all points satisfying a system of $(N-1)$ linearly independent linear equations. The equations can be represented by $(N-1)$ points in the space of parallel coordinates—see Fig. 4.3.

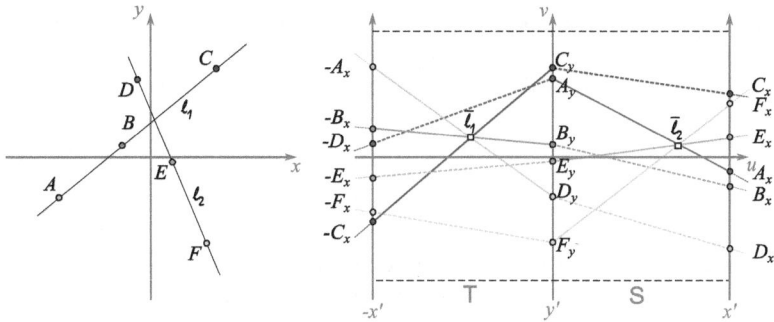

Fig. 4.4 *Left* Original $x - y$ space; *right* its PClines representation—the corresponding $\mathcal{T}\mathcal{S}$ space

Different spaces of parallel coordinates can be defined by using the axes in a different order. All these parameterizations are equivalent, but study of their relations is outside of the scope of this book (please refer to [1] instead).

4.2 PClines: The Line Parameterization

Since the parallel coordinates can serve as a point-to-line mapping, they can be used for parameterization of lines for the Hough transform. This section discusses this possibility and studies the properties of such a parameterization. The PClines parameterization was published by Dubská et al. [2]. A very similar approach was taken by El Mejdani et al. [3].

The PC representation of line $\ell : y = mx + b$ in the $u - v$ space is $\bar{\ell} = (d, b, 1 - m)_{\mathbb{P}^2}$, where d is the distance between the parallel axes x' and y'. The line's representation $\bar{\ell}$ lies between the axes x' and y' if and only if $-\infty < m < 0$. For $m = 1$, $\bar{\ell}$ is an ideal point (a point in infinity). For $m = 0$, $\bar{\ell}$ lies on the y' axis, for vertical lines ($m = \pm\infty$), $\bar{\ell}$ lies on the x' axis.

Besides this space of parallel coordinates x', y' (further referred to as *straight*, $\mathcal{S}$), we propose using a *twisted* ($\mathcal{T}$) system x', $-y'$, which is identical to the straight space, except that the y axis is inverted. In the twisted space, $\bar{\ell}$ is between the axes x' and $-y'$ if and only if $0 < m < \infty$. By combining the *straight* and the *twisted* spaces, the whole $\mathcal{T}\mathcal{S}$ plane can be constructed, as shown in Fig. 4.4. Figure 4.4 (left) shows the original $x - y$ image with points A, B, C, ..., F and two lines ℓ_1 and ℓ_2 coincident with the points. The origin of $x - y$ is placed into the middle of the image for convenience of the figures. Figure 4.4 (right) depicts the corresponding $\mathcal{T}\mathcal{S}$ space. Note that a finite part of the $u - v$ plane is sufficient:

$$-d \le u \le d,$$
$$-\max\left(\frac{W}{2}, \frac{H}{2}\right) \le v \le \max\left(\frac{W}{2}, \frac{H}{2}\right), \tag{4.2}$$

where W and H are the width and height of the input raster image, respectively.

Any line $\ell : y = mx + b$ is now represented either by $\bar{\ell}_S$ in the *straight* half or by $\bar{\ell}_T$ in the *twisted* part of the $u - v$ plane:

$$\bar{\ell}_S = (d, b, 1 - m)_{\mathbb{P}^2}, -\infty \le m \le 0,$$
$$\bar{\ell}_T = (-d, -b, 1 + m)_{\mathbb{P}^2}, 0 \le m \le \infty. \tag{4.3}$$

Consequently, any line ℓ has exactly one image $\bar{\ell}$ in the $\mathcal{TS}$ space; except for cases that $m = 0$ and $m = \pm\infty$, when $\bar{\ell}$ lies in both spaces on y' or x', respectively. That allows the $\mathcal{T}$ and $\mathcal{S}$ spaces to be "attached" one to another. Figure 4.4 illustrates the spaces attached along the x' axis. Attaching also the y' and $-y'$ axes results in an enclosed Möbius strip.

To detect the lines, the standard Hough transform procedure is performed: the $u - v$ space bounded by (4.2) is uniformly discretized into a matrix of accumulators; the input image is processed; and for all (or a selected subset) above-threshold pixels, a subset of the accumulators are incremented. In the case of PClines, two lines are rasterized for each input pixel: one in the straight half, one in the twisted half of the $\mathcal{TS}$ space. Horizontal coordinates of the lines' endpoints are fixed $\{0, d, -d\}$; vertical coordinates are directly the x, y and $-y$ coordinates of the original point.

It should be noted that for lines detected in the PClines space, the intersections with the $x - y$ image boundary are easily computed. The $\mathcal{TS}$ space can be divided into convex parts by four lines:

$$v = \pm\frac{1}{2}\left(\pm\frac{W + H}{d}u + W\right). \tag{4.4}$$

According to the affiliation of a detected maximum $\bar{\ell}$ to one of these parts, the edges of the input image intersected by line ℓ can be determined and the intersections with them efficiently computed using the properties of parallel coordinates.

4.3 Parameterization Accuracy

For inspection of the error in localization of a line, line's parameters can be selected arbitrarily. We will be considering the differences in θ and in ϱ mainly because these parameters are distributed evenly for different lines. Also, the $\theta - \varrho$ parameterization is very popular and frequently used, and thus benchmarking in these terms is reasonable.

The line localization error of the Hough transform can be predicted from the discretization density of the accumulator space. In the case of PClines, the density is proportional to the slope of functions $\theta(u)$ and $\varrho(u, v)$; higher slope means higher impact of the changes in u and v on the values of θ and ϱ and thus higher discretization error. The $\theta - \varrho$ line parameterization [4] can be viewed as ideal in this sense because

Fig. 4.5 Dependency of derivatives and discretization errors on u in S and T spaces. *Dashed*: First-order partial derivative of θ with respect to u (4.6). *Dash-dotted*: Second-order mixed derivatives of ϱ with respect to u and v (4.9). *Solid*: Combined error ε calculated from the derivatives. *Dotted*: Combined error calculated from derivatives with different discretization Δv

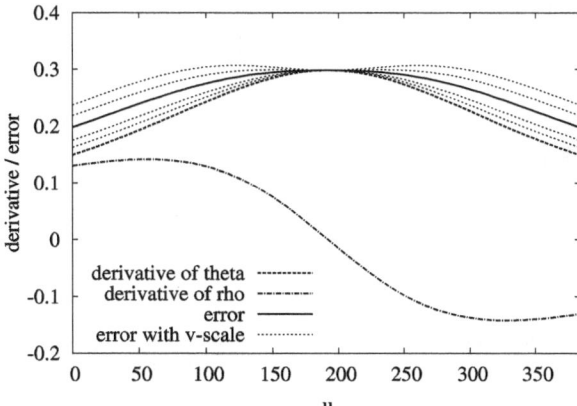

the slope is constant, so the discretization error is distributed uniformly across the Hough space.

In the S space, function $\theta(u)$ has its maximal slope when $u = d/2$, that is $m = -1$ (the situation is analogous in the T space):

$$\theta = \arctan\left(\frac{u}{d - u}\right),\tag{4.5}$$

$$\frac{\partial \theta}{\partial u} = \frac{d}{(d - u)^2 + u^2}.\tag{4.6}$$

Parameter θ is not dependent on v, so the discretization in the v axis has no influence on its error.

The ϱ parameter is a function of both u and v, as expressed in (4.7). For a given value of u, the discretization of $\varrho(u, v)$ is uniform across all v—see Eq. (4.8).

$$\varrho = \frac{vd}{\sqrt{(d - u)^2 + u^2}},\tag{4.7}$$

$$\frac{\partial \varrho}{\partial v} = \frac{d}{\sqrt{(d - u)^2 + u^2}}\tag{4.8}$$

The $\varrho(u, v)$ discretization error at any location in the TS space can therefore be expressed as

$$\frac{\partial^2 \varrho}{\partial u \partial v} = \frac{d(d - 2u)}{\sqrt{(d - u)^2 + u^2}^3}.\tag{4.9}$$

For convenience, two discretization error components ε_θ and ε_ϱ can be combined into one compound error $\varepsilon = \sqrt{\omega_\theta \varepsilon_\theta^2 + \omega_\varrho \varepsilon_\varrho^2}$ with weights ω_θ and ω_ϱ; this metric is used in the experimental evaluation. Figure 4.5 contains a visualization of Eqs. (4.6)

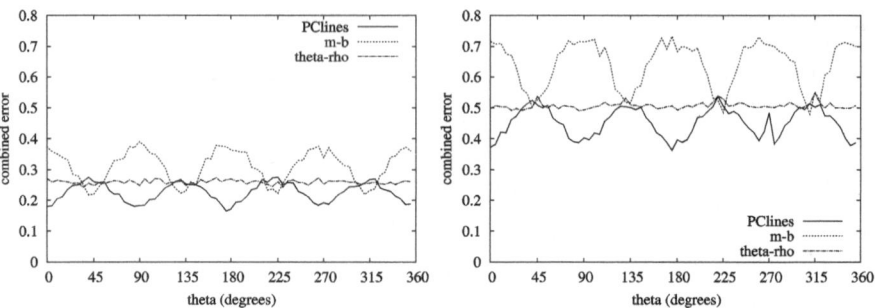

Fig. 4.6 Line localization error as depends on the slope of the line. The slopes are divided into bins 5° wide. *Left*: average error over all lines; *Right*: average error over 5 least accurate lines

and (4.9) (dashed), and several examples of the combined error (solid, dotted). One combination is drawn by the solid line as the "natural" one: $\omega_\theta = \omega_\varrho = 1$, discretization $\Delta u = \Delta v = 1$.

However, also other factors, different from the discretization of the Hough space, influence its accuracy. For example, the typical way of rasterizing the sinusoids in the $\theta - \varrho$ parameterization is incrementing one accumulator for one θ value, which results in a different density of rasterized accumulators in the Hough space, causing additional errors; these errors are not as predictable as the discretization errors. To cover all these factors, experimental evaluation has been carried out.

The accuracy of the PClines parameterization, the $\theta - \varrho$ parameterization, and the original Hough's parameterization $m - b$ was compared. Details of the evaluation can be found in [2]. Synthetic black&white images were used in the test. After the rasterization of the lines, every image was distorted by some noise pixels.

Figure 4.6 compares the errors of the three methods for lines with different θ generated within 5° wide intervals. For every interval of slopes, 100 images were generated, each with 1 line and 25,000 noise pixels. The average error of all lines (Fig. 4.6 left) and the average error of five least accurate lines (Fig. 4.6 right) was computed. The latter gives a pessimistic estimation of the errors.

References

1. Inselberg, A.: Parallel Coordinates: Visual Multidimensional Geometry and its Applications. Springer, New york (2009)
2. Dubská, M., Herout, A., Havel, J.: PClines—line detection using parallel coordinates. In: Proceedings of CVPR, (2011)
3. El Mejdani, S., Egli, R., Dubeau, F.: Old and new straight-line detectors: description and comparison. Pattern Recognit. **41**, 1845–1866 (2008). doi: DOIurl10.1016/j.patcog.2007.11.013 http://dl.acm.org/citation.cfm?id=1343128.1343451
4. Duda, R.O., Hart, P.E.: Use of the Hough transformation to detect lines and curves in pictures. Commun. ACM **15**(1), 11–15 (1972). http://doi.acm.org/10.1145/361237.361242

Chapter 5
Vanishing Points, Parallel Lines, Grids

This chapter will discuss the properties of perspectively projected rectangular grids and some observations fundamental for their detection. These grids are typically the edges in images containing checkerboards, QR codes, and similar patterns. It will also analyze the contents of the parameter space that results from the Hough transform of such patterns.

5.1 Projected Grids

The points on a set of mutually parallel lines can be expressed as

$$\mathbf{p} = \mathbf{p}_0 + s\mathbf{u} + t\mathbf{v}. \tag{5.1}$$

Either $\mathbf{u}$ or $\mathbf{v}$ can be used as the direction of the lines. One of s and t belongs to $\mathbb{R}$ and the other is generated by a step function

$$\text{step}_{\{s,t\}} : \mathbb{N}_0 \rightarrow \mathbb{R}. \tag{5.2}$$

For example, the step function

$$\text{step}_{\{s,t\}}(i) = ki \tag{5.3}$$

will generate equidistantly spaced lines such as edge lines in checkerboards or various matrix codes.

An infinite grid consists of two groups of mutually parallel lines. The points of the grid are generated by one or the other set of lines and can be described by equations:

$$\mathbf{p}_u(i, t) = \mathbf{p}_0 + \text{step}_s(i)\mathbf{u} + t\mathbf{v}, \, i \in \mathbb{N}_0, t \in \mathbb{R}, \tag{5.4}$$

$$\mathbf{p}_v(j, s) = \mathbf{p}_0 + \text{step}_t(j)\mathbf{v} + s\mathbf{u}, \, j \in \mathbb{N}_0, s \in \mathbb{R}. \tag{5.5}$$

A. Herout et al., *Real-Time Detection of Lines and Grids*,
SpringerBriefs in Computer Science, DOI: 10.1007/978-1-4471-4414-4_5,
© Adam Herout 2013

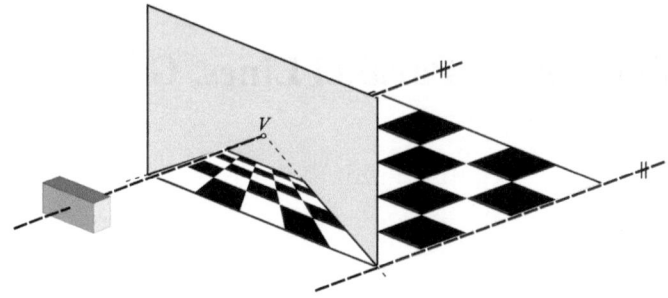

Fig. 5.1 Vanishing point V of a set of projected *parallel lines* is an intersection of the image plane and the *line* with the same direction passing through the *center* of projection

When the grid is viewed by a pinhole camera described by transformation/projection matrix $C = A[RT]$, Eq. (5.4) becomes

$$C\mathbf{p}_u(i,t) = C\mathbf{p}_0 + \text{step}_s(i)C\mathbf{u} + tC\mathbf{v} \tag{5.6}$$

and similarly for Eq. (5.5). Equation (5.6) shows that the step function is not distorted by the camera projection.

Equations (5.4) and (5.5) directly enumerate the homogeneous coordinates of points on the image plane with one important limitation. Vectors $\mathbf{p}$, $\mathbf{u}$, and $\mathbf{v}$ can no longer be multiplied by an arbitrary constant. Such a multiplication by arbitrary (nonzero) constant does not influence the interpretation of points in homogeneous coordinates. In this case, only the whole equation can be multiplied by a nonzero constant and the interpretation remains intact.

The grid has two vanishing points $\mathbf{p}_u(i,\infty) = \mathbf{p}_u^\infty$ and $\mathbf{p}_v^\infty$, which correspond to direction $\mathbf{u}$ and $\mathbf{v}$, respectively. A vanishing point is an intersection of the image plane and a line parallel to the grid lines that passes through the center of projection (i.e., the camera position—Fig. 5.1).

The vanishing point is a point on a line at infinity and its Cartesian coordinates are

$$\mathbf{p}_u^\infty = \lim_{t \to \infty} \frac{\mathbf{p}_u(i,t)_{xy}}{\mathbf{p}_u(i,t)_w} = \frac{\frac{\mathrm{d}}{\mathrm{d}t}\mathbf{p}_u(i,t)_{xy}}{\frac{\mathrm{d}}{\mathrm{d}t}\mathbf{p}_u(i,t)_w} = \frac{\mathbf{v}_{xy}}{\mathbf{v}_w}. \tag{5.7}$$

Therefore, $\mathbf{p}_u^\infty \equiv \mathbf{v}$ and $\mathbf{p}_v^\infty \equiv \mathbf{u}$.

As the resulting point can be safely multiplied by any nonzero constant without any change, the Eqs. (5.4) and (5.5) can be interpreted as a weighted average of a starting point and two vanishing points. Because of the fixed proportion of $\mathbf{p}_0$, $\mathbf{u}$, and $\mathbf{v}$, the grid has 8 degrees of freedom.

Grid Lines

Homogeneous coordinates of the grid lines can be calculated from two points of the line at t_0 and t_1, with $t_0 \neq t_1$.

$$\mathbf{l}_u(i) = \mathbf{p}_u(i, t_0) \times \mathbf{p}_u(i, t_1) = (t_1 - t_0)(\mathbf{p}_0 \times \mathbf{v} + \text{step}_s(i)\mathbf{u} \times \mathbf{v}) \qquad (5.8)$$

The proof can be found in Appendix D. Because multiplication by a nonzero constant does not change the line and $t_0 \neq t_1$, the term $(t_1 - t_0)$ can be ignored. Then, the line becomes a weighted sum of two lines

$$\mathbf{l}_u(i) = \mathbf{l}_u^0 + \text{step}_s(i)\mathbf{l}^\infty \qquad (5.9)$$

and similarly for the lines in the other direction. The "first" line $\mathbf{l}_u^0$ connects $\mathbf{p}_0$ and the vanishing point $\mathbf{v}$ and the line $\mathbf{l}^\infty$ connects both the vanishing points. As the omitted subscript indicates, line $\mathbf{l}^\infty$ is common for both the directions and it is called the *horizon*. The horizon is an intersection of the image plane and the plane parallel to the grid that passes through the center of projection. As in the case of the equations for the points on the lines, the constant multiplication is possible only for the complete equation.

A grid in the image can be fully specified in two ways. One way is by a pair of vanishing points $\mathbf{u}$ and $\mathbf{v}$ and the "first" point $\mathbf{p}_0$ using Eqs. (5.4) and (5.5). The other uses two "first" lines $\mathbf{l}_u^0$ and $\mathbf{l}_v^0$ and the common horizon $\mathbf{l}^\infty$. Because these vectors must be scaled together, the grid has not nine but only eight degrees of freedom.

5.2 Vanishing Points in PTLM and Other Parameterizations

When a grid is detected by the Hough transform, each grid point is transformed to a curve and each grid line corresponds to a point in the parameter space. For simplicity, the line parameterizations will now be limited to point-to-line mappings. The slope-intercept parameterization and the PClines belong to this class.

When the grid points and lines are mapped by PTLM F and a corresponding LTPM (line-to-point mapping) F^{-T}, Eqs. (5.4) and (5.9) become

$$F\mathbf{p}_u(i, t) = F\mathbf{p}_0 + \text{step}_s(i)F\mathbf{u} + tF\mathbf{v}, \qquad (5.10)$$

$$F^{-T}\mathbf{l}_u(i) = F^{-T}\mathbf{l}_u^0 + \text{step}_s(i)F^{-T}\mathbf{l}^\infty. \qquad (5.11)$$

The images of the lines of the grid (i.e. points in the parameter space) lie on the images of the vanishing points (lines in the parameter space). The images of the vanishing points intersect at the image of the horizon line. When the vanishing points do not lie on the ideal line (line in infinity), the distances between the images of the grid lines shrink, as they approach the image of the horizon. This becomes more

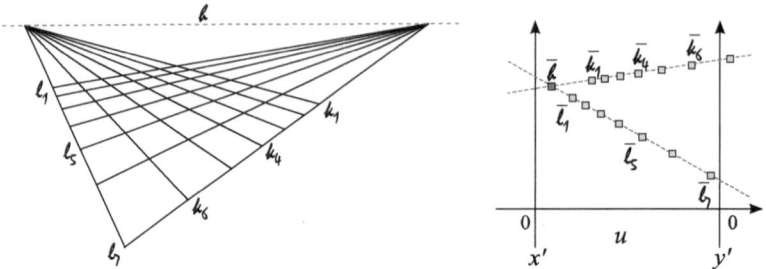

Fig. 5.2 A grid under perspective projection and its representation in a point-to-line mapping. In the Cartesian coordinates, both *groups of lines* converge to a *horizon line*. In the mapping, these *lines* are represented by *collinear points* and converge to a *point* representing the *horizon line*

obvious with an increased perspective distortion of the grid. Figure 5.2 illustrates these relations. It should be noted that the image shows an extreme situation. In most practical situations, the image of the horizon will be far from the stored portion of the parameter space and the images of the vanishing points will be in separate halves of the parameter space.

In the $\theta-\varrho$ parameterization, the vanishing points do not correspond to lines, but to sinusoid curves. However, when the vanishing point is "far enough" from the image area, the curve representing the vanishing point is "close to linear" and it can be approximated by a line with a practically acceptable error.

An alternative approach to detection of the vanishing point can be RANSAC [2] or solving of a linear system. Theoretically, only two lines are required for the localization of the vanishing point. However, the lines are detected with an error and a small error in the line's angle can lead to a large error in the position of the vanishing point. The vanishing point location can be detected more precisely from multiple lines. Given a set of lines $\{\mathbf{l}_1, \ldots, \mathbf{l}_N\}$, the vanishing point $\mathbf{v}$ can be found by solving the following equation:

$$L\mathbf{v}^T = \begin{pmatrix} \mathbf{l}_1 \\ \vdots \\ \mathbf{l}_N \end{pmatrix} \mathbf{v}^T = \mathbf{0}^T, \tag{5.12}$$

which just means that every line passes through the point $\mathbf{v}$. When there are more than two lines, the system is overspecified (has more equations than unknowns). Of course, because of unprecisely detected lines, no accurate solution exists. The vanishing point must be found as a least square error solution or in a similar manner.

When the line coordinates are interpreted as a 3-D vector space without an origin (each line through the origin represents one line in 2-D), the vanishing points correspond to the hyperplanes through the origin. This is the geometrical meaning of Eq. (5.12). The vanishing point can therefore be found by hyperplane fitting, for

Fig. 5.3 Cross-ratio of four
intersections is identical for all
lines, i.e. $(\mathbf{p}_a, \mathbf{p}_b; \mathbf{p}_c, \mathbf{p}_d) =$
$(\mathbf{p}'_a, \mathbf{p}'_b; \mathbf{p}'_c, \mathbf{p}'_d) =$
$(\mathbf{p}''_a, \mathbf{p}''_b; \mathbf{p}''_c, \mathbf{p}''_d)$

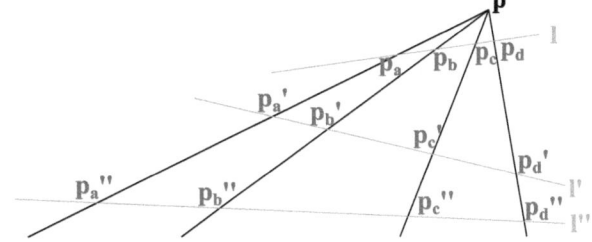

example by uncentered PCA. By eigendecomposition of the correlation matrix

$$C = \left(\mathbf{l}_1^T \ldots \mathbf{l}_N^T\right) \begin{pmatrix} \mathbf{l}_1 \\ \vdots \\ \mathbf{l}_N \end{pmatrix}, \tag{5.13}$$

three principal components are found. The component with the least variance (eigen-value) is the hyperplane normal and a good approximation of the desired vanishing point.

5.3 Cross-Ratio Under Perspective Projection

One of the basic properties of the perspective projection is invariance of the cross-ratio. In general, the cross-ratio is a numeric association between a 4-tuple of collinear points, defined as:

$$(\mathbf{p}_a, \mathbf{p}_b; \mathbf{p}_c, \mathbf{p}_d) = \frac{|\mathbf{p}_a\mathbf{p}_c| : |\mathbf{p}_b\mathbf{p}_c|}{|\mathbf{p}_a\mathbf{p}_d| : |\mathbf{p}_b\mathbf{p}_d|}, \tag{5.14}$$

where $|\mathbf{p}_x\mathbf{p}_y|$ is the signed distance of points $\mathbf{p}_x, \mathbf{p}_y$. Invariance under perspective means that for arbitrary four lines with a common point $\mathbf{v}$, the cross-ratio of inter-sections with a line $\mathbf{l}$ is the same for any arbitrary line (see Fig. 5.3) [1].

After projecting a 3D plane which contains two or more groups of mutually parallel lines, each group of lines converges into a vanishing point. All vanishing points lie on a common line—the horizon [1]. In the case of planar grids or matrix codes projected perspectively from a 3D space to two dimensions, there are two groups of parallel lines, all coincident with a common plane. Two corresponding vanishing points $\mathbf{u}, \mathbf{v}$ define the horizon line. Intersections of any line parallel to the horizon and the projections of *equally* spaced parallel lines are always equally spaced (see Fig. 5.4). It means that for an ordered set of equidistant lines $\mathbf{l}_1, \mathbf{l}_2, \mathbf{l}_3, \ldots, \mathbf{l}_n$, the cross-ratio of lines $\mathbf{l}_a, \mathbf{l}_b, \mathbf{l}_c, \mathbf{l}_d$ is:

$$(\mathbf{l}_a, \mathbf{l}_b; \mathbf{l}_c, \mathbf{l}_d) = \frac{(a-c):(b-c)}{(a-d):(b-d)}. \tag{5.15}$$

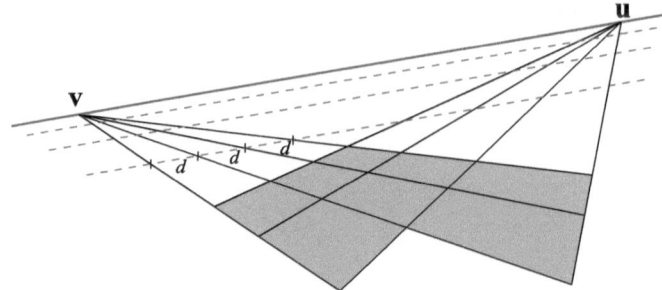

Fig. 5.4 Two groups of coplanar uniformly spaced parallel lines projected by a perspective projection and their vanishing points **u**, **v**. *Dashed lines* are parallel to the horizon. Intersections of each *dashed line* with the *thick lines* are uniformly spaced

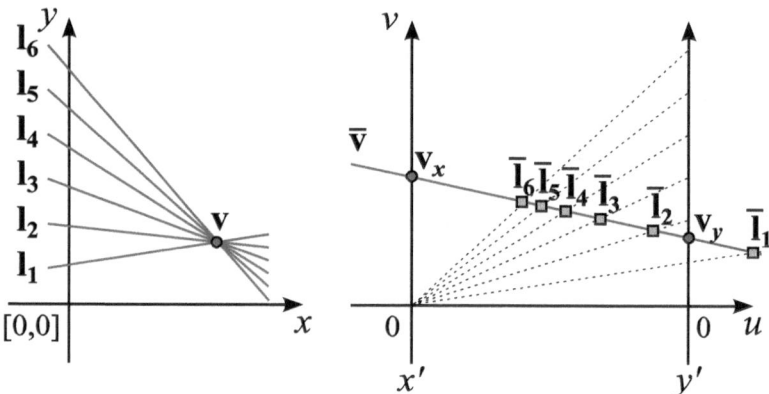

Fig. 5.5 Pencil of lines in (*left*) Cartesian coordinate system; (*right*) Parallel coordinates

As mentioned above, images of perspectively projected parallel lines in point-to-line mappings lie on a common line—the representation of the corresponding vanishing point. A group of *equally* spaced coplanar parallel lines and their intersections with any line parallel to the horizon are also equally spaced (see Fig. 5.4). This can be used for deriving relations between the points representing the projected (equally spaced) lines in the parallel coordinates. Consider a group of lines projected to a 2D image plane: $l_1, l_2, \ldots, l_k$. Its image in parallel coordinates is a set of points $\bar{l}_1, \bar{l}_2, \ldots, \bar{l}_k$ that lie on a line $\bar{v}$, the representation of their vanishing point (see Fig. 5.5).

The relation between the representations can be expressed by the value of the cross-ratio, which is for any set of lines $\mathbf{l}_a, \mathbf{l}_b, \mathbf{l}_c, \mathbf{l}_d$ evaluated as follows:

$$\frac{|\bar{\mathbf{l}}_c\bar{\mathbf{l}}_a| : |\bar{\mathbf{l}}_c\bar{\mathbf{l}}_b|}{|\bar{\mathbf{l}}_d\bar{\mathbf{l}}_a| : |\bar{\mathbf{l}}_d\bar{\mathbf{l}}_b|} = \frac{(c-a) : (c-b)}{(d-a) : (d-b)}, \tag{5.16}$$

where a, b, c, d are the indices of the four lines within the sorted set of lines $\bar{\mathbf{l}}_1, \bar{\mathbf{l}}_2, \ldots, \bar{\mathbf{l}}_k$ and $|\bar{\mathbf{l}}_i\bar{\mathbf{l}}_j|$ is the distance of the points representing the lines in the parallel coordinates. Because these representations lie on a straight line, the equation also holds for separate u and v coordinates of the lines' representations (u, v are the Cartesian coordinates within the plane used by the parallel coordinates—see Chap. 4). This means that for arbitrary $\mathbf{l}_a, \mathbf{l}_b, \mathbf{l}_c$ with known $(b-a)$ and $(c-b)$, it is possible to derive the rest of the uniformly spaced parallel lines.

5.4 Detection of Grids Using PClines

For the detection of a grid in parallel coordinates, two methods are introduced in the following text. These methods use the same way for accumulation of the Hough space, but they differ in the detection of perspectively projected parallel lines in the accumulated space. The first one is based on verification and ranking of hypotheses about the set of lines based on a known value of the cross-ratio. The second one uses backprojection and finds equally spaced points representing the lines.

The input for the algorithm (Algorithm 3) is an image with a grid. First, the edge points are detected and their gradients are estimated by using, for example, the Sobel operator (line 4). A histogram of oriented gradients with a small number of bins ($N_G = 8, 12, 16$) is built together with a list of edges that voted for the bin (line 6). Since a regular grid is expected to be present in the image, two main peaks can be detected in the histogram (line 9). These two peaks, roughly 90° degrees apart, represent two main orientations in the image (Fig. 5.6a).

The horizontal position of a point in the $\mathcal{TS}$ space corresponds to the slope of the line represented by this point. That means that only two small parts of the $\mathcal{TS}$ space can be accumulated, instead of the whole space (Fig. 5.6b). That leads to a significant memory and computational reduction (line 13–18).

Each of the accumulated stripes of the $\mathcal{TS}$ space is accumulated either in the *straight* or in the *twisted* manner as a whole. After accumulation, each stripe of the Hough space contains collinear maxima which have to be detected as a whole. Two approaches are discussed in detail further (Sects. 5.4.1 and 5.4.2). Let us suppose that the sets of lines are already detected. The grid can be used for calculating the perspective projection and/or calibrating the camera. Alternatively, the input image is sampled in the middle of the cells of the grid and any encoded information (as in the case of the QR codes) is extracted.

Algorithm 3 HT for detecting sets of perspectively projected equidistant lines using PClines.

Input: Input image I with dimensions I_w, I_h, Hough space dimensions H_u, H_v, number of edge bins N_G

Output: Detected two sets of perspectively projected equidistant lines $L_s = \{l_1, l_2, \ldots, l_n\}, L_t = \{k_1, k_2, \ldots, k_n\}$

1: $G(n_\theta) \leftarrow \emptyset, \forall n_\theta \in \{0, \ldots, N_G\} \wedge n_\theta \in \mathbb{N}_0$

2: **for all** $x \in \{1, \ldots, I_w\}, y \in \{1, \ldots, I_h\}$ **do**

3:     **if** $I(x, y)$ **is edge then**

4:         estimate its gradient g_i

5:         $i = \lfloor \frac{g_i}{\pi} * N_G \rfloor$

6:         $G(i) = G(i) \cup I(x, y)$

7:     **end if**

8: **end for**

9: $s : |G(s)| = max(|G(i)|), i \in \{0, \ldots, N_G\}$

10: $t : |G(t)| = max(|G(i)|), i \in \{0, \ldots, N_G\} - \{s\}$

11: $H_s(u, v) \leftarrow 0, u \in 1, \ldots, H_u \wedge v \in 1, \ldots H_v$

12: $H_t(u, v) \leftarrow 0, u \in 1, \ldots, H_u \wedge v \in 1, \ldots H_v$

13: **for all** $I(x, y) \in G(s)$ **do**

14:     **accumulate** line in H_s

15: **end for**

16: **for all** $I(x, y) \in G(t)$ **do**

17:     **accumulate** line in H_t

18: **end for**

19: get L_s from H_s

20: get L_t from H_t

21: **return** L_s, L_t

5.4.1 Detection by Using the Cross-Ratio

As mentioned in Sect. 5.3, the value of the cross-ratio for a quadruple of the points in the parallel coordinates is equal to the cross-ratio of the lines represented by these points. This can be used for the detection of a pencil of lines with a known distribution, for example equidistant lines under a perspective projection. The pencil of lines is in the parallel coordinate system represented by a set of collinear points.

The detection algorithm (Algorithm 4) requires a filled Hough space as its input. First, several highest local maxima are detected (set M, line 3). The maxima, in an ideal case, correspond to the most significant lines on the grid. For uniquely determining the perspective projection, three lines with known indices (or mutual distances) are required. Therefore, triplets $\{p_a, p_b, p_c\}$ are selected from the set M (line 6). Suppose these three points lie on a common line—the vanishing point. Using, for example, a linear square regression for calculating the line l best fitting points $\{p_a, p_b, p_c\}$, a hypothetical vanishing point is obtained (line 7). If the fitting error is over a given threshold, i.e. the points are not collinear, the hypothesis is rejected. Even when the hypothesis is not rejected, points p_a, p_b, p_c may not precisely lie on

(a) **(b)**

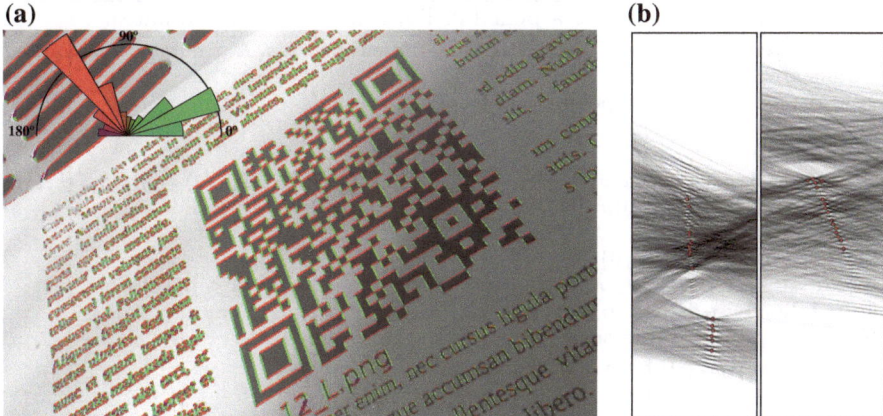

Fig. 5.6 Edge extraction and accumulation. **a** Original QRcode image with detected edges. In the *left-top* corner, histogram of edge orientations—two peaks can be found and only the relevant edges are selected and used for **b** accumulation of two parts of the accumulator space. The *red dots* correspond to maxima in the Hough spaces

a line, because of discretization, accumulation, or detection errors. However, the ideal case expects maxima on a common line. Therefore, a projection of the points $\{\mathbf{p}_a, \mathbf{p}_b, \mathbf{p}_c\}$ to a line $\mathbf{l}$ is made (line 8). In most cases, the points are very close to the line, so the projection in the horizontal direction is sufficiently accurate instead of perpendicular projection which is more costly.

For a full derivation of the perspective, the number of points on the line $\mathbf{l}$ within the sorted projected points $\mathbf{p}'_a, \mathbf{p}'_b, \mathbf{p}'_c$ are needed. These points represent the lines of the grid between the lines $\mathbf{l}'_a, \mathbf{l}'_b, \mathbf{l}'_c$, corresponding to points $\mathbf{p}'_a, \mathbf{p}'_b, \mathbf{p}'_c$. From this information, indices of the lines can be defined and used in Eq. (5.16). The points are counted as the number of local maxima on the line $\mathbf{l}$ between $\mathbf{p}'_a\mathbf{p}'_b$ and $\mathbf{p}'_b\mathbf{p}'_c$ (lines 9, 10 of the algorithm). Let us consider $\mathbf{p}'_b$ as the 0th maximum, which makes $\mathbf{p}'_a$ the $(-N_{ab} - 1)$th and $\mathbf{p}'_c$ the $(N_{bc} + 1)$th maximum (lines 11–13). The coordinates for the ith maximum or minimum can be now determined using Eq. (5.16) (line 18). The equation can be used separately on both (u and v) coordinates or only on one of them and the other is calculated as a point on line $\mathbf{l}$ with one known coordinate. The confidence score of the hypothesis about the vanishing point and the distribution of the lines depends on the values in the Hough space on the positions of the computed maxima (line 19). The score can be modified by taking into account also the positions of the minima (lines passing through the centers of the cells in the grid) and expecting low values at these positions. The algorithm returns the set of points of the hypothesis with the highest score (lines 21–25) (Fig. 5.7).

Algorithm 4 Detection of a pencil of lines in Parallel coordinates.

Input: Accumulated Hough space H with dimensions H_u, H_v; number of required
    init maxima $N_M \geq 3$.
Output: Set of collinear points P in Hough space.
  1: $M = \emptyset$
  2: **for** $i = 0 \rightarrow N_M$ **do**
  3:    $M = M \cup (u,v), (u,v) \in \{0, \ldots, H_u\} \times \{0, \ldots, H_v\} \wedge H(u,v) = max(H(k,l))$:
      $\forall (p,q) \in M : |(k,l)(p,q)| > \delta$
  4: **end for**
  5: $\mathcal{H} = \{\mathcal{H}^P, \mathcal{H}^s\} = \{\emptyset, 0\}$
  6: **for all** $\{\mathbf{p}_a, \mathbf{p}_b, \mathbf{p}_c\} \subset M \wedge \mathbf{p}_a \neq \mathbf{p}_b \neq \mathbf{p}_c \wedge \mathbf{p}_a(v) < \mathbf{p}_b(v) < \mathbf{p}_c(v)$ **do**
  7:    l: line best fitting $\{\mathbf{p}_a, \mathbf{p}_b, \mathbf{p}_c\}$
  8:    $\{\mathbf{p}'_a, \mathbf{p}'_b, \mathbf{p}'_c\}$: projections of points $\{\mathbf{p}_a, \mathbf{p}_b, \mathbf{p}_c\}$ to line l
  9:    $N_{ab} = |\{p : p \in l \wedge p \text{ is local maximum} \wedge p \in \overline{\mathbf{p}'_a \mathbf{p}'_b}\}|$
10:    $N_{bc} = |\{p : p \in l \wedge p \text{ is local maximum} \wedge p \in \overline{\mathbf{p}'_b \mathbf{p}'_c}\}|$
11:    $a = -N_{ab} - 1$
12:    $b = 0$
13:    $c = N_{bc} + 1$
14:    $\mathcal{H}_{abc} = \{\emptyset, 0\}$
15:    **for** $i = d \rightarrow t$ **do**
16:       $\alpha = (c - a)(i - b)$
17:       $\beta = (c - b)(i - a)$
18:       $m_i = \dfrac{\alpha \mathbf{p}'_c \mathbf{p}'_a - \beta \mathbf{p}'_b \mathbf{p}'_c + (\beta - \alpha)\mathbf{p}'_a \mathbf{p}'_b}{\beta \mathbf{p}'_a - \alpha \mathbf{p}'_b + (\alpha - \beta)\mathbf{p}'_c}$
19:       $\mathcal{H}_{abc} = \{\mathcal{H}^P_{abc} \cup m_i, \mathcal{H}^s_{abc} + H(m_i)\}$
20:    **end for**
21:    **if** $\mathcal{H}^s_{abc} > \mathcal{H}^s$ **then**
22:       $\mathcal{H} = \mathcal{H}_{abc}$
23:    **end if**
24: **end for**
25: **return** $\mathcal{H}^P$

5.4.2 Detection of Grids by Inverse Projection

A grid under perspective projection P can be backprojected with an inverse transformation P^- so that the lines in each direction are again parallel. In parallel coordinates it means a transformation of the space where the points representing the lines are equidistant and lie on a line parallel to the axes (i.e. the intersections determining the coordinates of the vanishing point are in infinity). The matrix of such a projection can be fully defined up to the scale by two vanishing points $\mathbf{u}$ and $\mathbf{v}$ corresponding to two main directions of the grid's lines. Considering $(1, 0, 0)_{\mathbb{P}^2}$ and $(0, 1, 0)_{\mathbb{P}^2}$ as these two main orientations, the projection matrix P can be determined from the equation $\mathbf{a}_p = \mathbf{a}P$ as follows:

(a) **(b)**

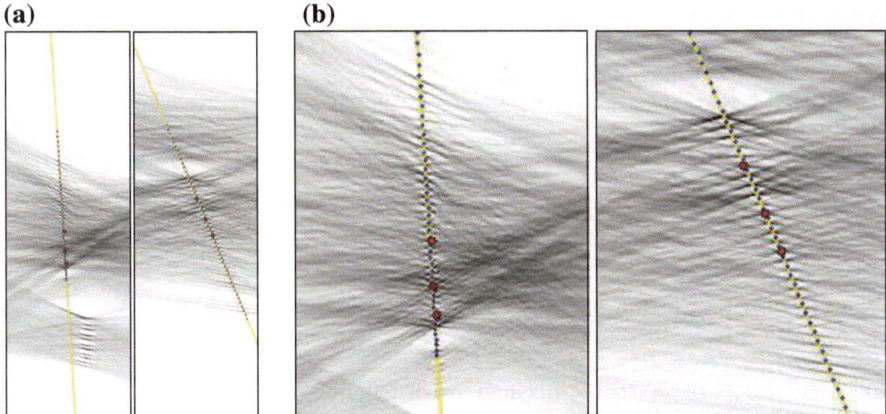

Fig. 5.7 Triplets of maxima (*red dots*) with the corresponding line used for vanishing point estimation (*yellow line*). *Blue dots* represent the estimated minima, where low values are expected. **a** The whole accumulator stripes; **b** zoom to selected parts of the accumulator stripes

$$\mathbf{u} = (U_x, U_y, 1)_{\mathbb{P}2} = (1, 0, 0)_{\mathbb{P}2} P$$
$$\mathbf{v} = (V_x, V_y, 1)_{\mathbb{P}2} = (0, 1, 0)_{\mathbb{P}2} P$$
$$\mathbf{o} = (1, 1, 1)_{\mathbb{P}2} = (1, 1, 1)_{\mathbb{P}2} P$$
$$P = \begin{pmatrix} U_x & U_y & 1 \\ V_x & V_y & 1 \\ 1 & 1 & 1 \end{pmatrix} \tag{5.17}$$

In practice, it means that an input image with a captured grid can by projected by transformation P^- so that the lines are parallel and aligned with the image sides. To find such a matrix P^-, both the vanishing points $\mathbf{u}$ and $\mathbf{v}$ can be used.

Consider now the situation in the parallel coordinates. As shown in Fig. 5.2, images of perspectively projected lines lie on a single line. This line in parallel coordinates is a point in the Cartesian coordinates common for all lines, i.e. the vanishing point $\mathbf{u}$. The second group of lines, originally coplanar with the first one, also creates a collinear set of points on a common line—the representation of vanishing point $\mathbf{v}$. Lines corresponding to $\mathbf{u}$ and $\mathbf{v}$ intersect at point $\bar{\mathbf{h}}$. The point $\bar{\mathbf{h}}$ in parallel coordinates is a line $\mathbf{h}$ in Cartesian coordinates which passes through $\mathbf{u}$ and $\mathbf{v}$—the line called *horizon*. Both the groups of points in parallel coordinates converge to point $\bar{\mathbf{h}}$. Using transformation P^- in the parallel coordinates, the points representing the lines are equidistant and they can be easily detected.

Algorithm 5 Detection of a pencil of lines in Parallel coordinates.

Input: Two accumulated Hough space H_s and H_t with dimensions H_u, H_v; number
   of required init maxima $N_M \geq 3$.
Output: Set of collinear points P_s and P_t in Hough space H_s, respectively H_t.
1: **for all** $H \in H_s, H_t$ **do**
2:    $M = \emptyset$
3:    **for** $i = 0 \to N_M$ **do**
4:       $M = M \cup (u,v), (u,v) \in \{0, \dots, H_u\} \times \{0, \dots, H_v\} \wedge H(u,v) = max(H(k,l)) : \forall(p,q) \in M : |(k,l)(p,q)| > \delta$
5:    **end for**
6: **end for**
7: $\mathbf{l}_s, \mathbf{l}_t$: lines best fitting M_s, resp. M_t
8: **for all** $\mathbf{l} \in \mathbf{l}_s, \mathbf{l}_t$ **do**
9:    $\{\mathbf{n}_i\}_{i=0}^{H_v} : \mathbf{n}_i = H(x,i) \wedge (x,i) \in \mathbf{l}$
10:   $\{\mathbf{n}'_i\}_{i=0}^{H_v} : \mathbf{n}'_i = f(\mathbf{n}_i) \wedge$ maxima are distributed uniformly, see Eq. (5.22)
11:   $\{a_i\}_{i=0}^{H_v} : a_i = \sum\limits_{j=0}^{H_v - i} \mathbf{n}_j \mathbf{n}_{j+i}$
12:   $I = max(a_i) \wedge i > \epsilon$
13:   $\{b_i\}_{i=0}^{I} : b_i = \sum\limits_{j\%I=i} \mathbf{n}_j$
14:   $F = max(b_i)$
15:   $P' = \{\forall \, \mathbf{n}_i : i\%I = F\}$
16:   $P = f^{-1}(P')$
17: **end for**
18: **return** P_s and P_t

The whole algorithm is shown in Algorithm 5. As the input, the algorithm expects
two accumulated stripes of the Hough space using PClines (Algorithm 3). First, a
set of maxima is searched for each part (line 4). The maxima in the accumulators
represent dominant lines in the input image. Assume these lines are perspectively
projected parallel lines so that in the Hough space, they lie on a common line. This
line can be found, for example, by RANSAC [2] or by least squares ($\mathbf{l}_{us}$ and $\mathbf{l}_{vt}$ line
7 of the algorithm). In each part, one line is found representing one vanishing point
in the processed image.

$$\bar{\mathbf{u}} = \mathbf{l}_{us} = (-1, m_u, b_u)$$
$$\bar{\mathbf{v}} = \mathbf{l}_{vt} = (-1, m_v, b_v) \tag{5.18}$$

The lines are parametrized according to the u–v coordinate system from Fig. 4.4.
Further, the lines are processed separately for each part. The goal is to get the maxima
on the line distributed uniformly by using a nonuniform sampling along the line. To
get the nth sample, the algorithm uses the orientation of the slope. The remapping
equation depends mainly on the position of the horizon, i.e. the line incident with
points $\mathbf{l}_u$ and $\mathbf{l}_v$. In parallel coordinates it means intersection of lines $\bar{\mathbf{u}}$ and $\bar{\mathbf{v}}$. Because
lines $\bar{\mathbf{u}}$ and $\bar{\mathbf{v}}$ can be found in parts of the Hough space from both the $\mathcal{T}$ or $\mathcal{S}$ spaces,
variable σ defines where each line belongs (Eq. (5.19)).

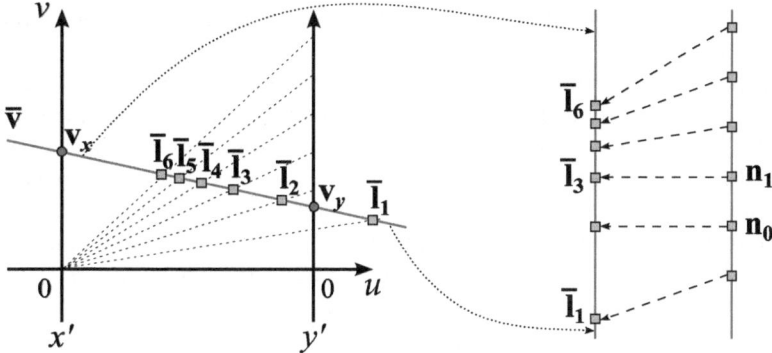

Fig. 5.8 Sampling of the values along the vanishing point. *Dashed arrows* show the couples of input-image points

$$\sigma(\mathbf{x}) = \begin{cases} 1 & x \in \mathcal{S} \\ -1 & x \in \mathcal{T} \end{cases} \tag{5.19}$$

The horizon is then calculated using $\overline{\mathbf{u}}$ and $\overline{\mathbf{v}}$ and is characterized by the tangent of its orientation (Eq. (5.20), Appendix C).

$$t = \frac{\begin{vmatrix} m_u & m_v & 0 \\ 1 & 1 & 1 \\ \sigma(\overline{\mathbf{u}})b_u & \sigma(\overline{\mathbf{v}})b_v & d \end{vmatrix}}{\begin{vmatrix} m_u & m_v \\ b_u & b_v \end{vmatrix}} \tag{5.20}$$

The main goal is to sample the values along the vanishing point in a way to get the maxima distributed uniformly (Fig. 5.8). First, two points are fixed to have the same distance in the original Hough space and in the new sampling (Eq. (5.21)).

$$\mathbf{n}_0 = (u_0, v_0, 1)_{\mathbb{P}^2}$$
$$\mathbf{n}_1 = (u_1, v_1, 1)_{\mathbb{P}^2} \tag{5.21}$$

Now, for each point $\mathbf{n}_i$ along the 1D resampled vector there is a corresponding point in the Hough space with coordinates $(u_i, v_1, 1)\mathbb{P}^2$ defined as:

$$\mathbf{n}_i = (u_i, v_i, 1)$$
$$u_i = \frac{(-t - \sigma(\mathbf{n}_i))u_1u_0 + d(iu_1 - (i-1)u_0)}{(-t - \sigma(\mathbf{n}_i))(iu_0 - (i-1)u_1) + d}$$
$$v_i = \frac{(-t - \sigma(\mathbf{n}_i))(iu_0v_1 - (i-1)u_1v_0) + d(iv_1 - (i-1)v_0)}{(-t - \sigma(\mathbf{n}_i))(iu_0 - (i-1)u_1) + d}, \tag{5.22}$$

where $i \in \mathbb{R}$ and d is the distance between the parallel lines (for a proof see Appendix C).

By a given discretization of i, the 1D vector with a required resolution is sampled (line 10). To find the frequency of the maxima, autocorrelation of the sequence is used (line 11). The maximal value of the autocorrelation (omitting the first few values) defines the distances between the maxima (line 12). For getting the positions of all maxima, the position of at least one maximum is required (line 13). Using the uniform distance and one maximum, the positions of the rest maxima are derived (line 15). These indices are again used in Eq. (5.22) and the resulting $(u_j, v_j, 1)$ are the positions of the maxima in the Hough space.

Reference

1. Hartley, R.I., Zisserman, A.: Multiple View Geometry in Computer Vision, 2 edn. Cambridge University Press, (2004). ISBN: 0521540518
2. Fischler, M.A., Bolles, R.C.: Random sample consensus: a paradigm for model fitting with applications to image analysis and automated cartography, Commun. ACM. 24(6), 381–395 (1981)

Chapter 6
Efficient Implementation of PClines

This chapter discusses possibilities of implementation of the PClines-based detectors on graphics processors. Section 6.2 deals with an OpenGL implementation of the line detector [1]. The OpenGL implementation can be executed on various graphics devices, including advanced graphics chips for mobile phones. Since PClines is based on rasterization of lines (in contrast to the $\theta-\varrho$ parameterization, which requires rasterization of sinusoids), the standard and very efficient graphics rasterization operations can be used. Section 6.3 describes an approach to line detection based on the Hough transform designed for CUDA and OpenCL. This detector can also be implemented on general hardware, such as the FPGA or ASIC chips, because it requires a small buffer of read-write memory. Also, thanks to the nature of the PClines parameterization, it can be implemented completely without the use of floating-point operations.

6.1 General Considerations

As mentioned in Sect. 2.1, the edge orientation can be used to reduce the modified portion of the parameter space for every edge point. O'Gorman and Clowes [2] improved the basic $\theta-\varrho$ parameterization with their idea of not accumulating values for all discretized values of θ, but for a single value of θ, instead. The appropriate θ for a point can be obtained from the gradient of the detected edge at this point [3]. With the $\mathcal{TS}$ parameterization, the approach is similar.

One common way to calculate the local gradient direction of the image intensity is by using the Sobel operator. The Sobel kernels for convolution are as follows: $S_x = [1, 2, 1]^T \cdot [1, 0, -1]$ and $S_y = [1, 0, -1]^T \cdot [1, 2, 1]$. Using these convolution kernels, two gradient values G_x and G_y can be obtained for any discrete location in the input image. Based on these, the gradient's direction is $\theta = \arctan(G_y/G_x)$.

A. Herout et al., *Real-Time Detection of Lines and Grids*,
SpringerBriefs in Computer Science, DOI: 10.1007/978-1-4471-4414-4_6,
© Adam Herout 2013

Fig. 6.1 Dependency of u on θ: nonlinear, but close to linear, so the error in the "radius" is small and acceptable

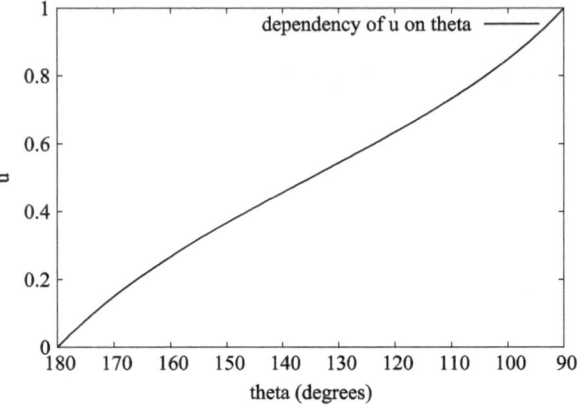

The line's inclination in the slope-intercept parameterization $m - b$ is related to θ:

$$m = -\tan\frac{1}{\theta}. \tag{6.1}$$

The slope m of line ℓ defines the u coordinate of the line's image $\bar{\ell}$ in the $\mathcal{TS}$ space: $u = d/(1 - m)$ for $\mathcal{S}$ space and $u = -d/(1 + m)$ for $\mathcal{T}$ space. When $\bar{\ell}$ is in the $\mathcal{S}$ space,

$$u_{\mathcal{S}} = d\frac{1}{1 - m} = d\frac{1}{1 + \tan\theta^{-1}} = d\frac{G_y}{G_x + G_y} \tag{6.2}$$

and similarly in the $\mathcal{T}$ space

$$u_{\mathcal{T}} = d\frac{G_y}{G_x - G_y}. \tag{6.3}$$

The u coordinate can be expressed independently of the location of $\bar{\ell}$ as

$$u = d\frac{G_y}{G_x + \mathrm{sgn}(G_x)|G_y|}. \tag{6.4}$$

It should be noted that contrary to the "standard" θ–ϱ parameterization, no goniometric operation is needed to compute the horizontal position of the ideal gradient in the accumulator space. In order to avoid errors caused by noise and by the discrete nature of the input image, accumulators within a suitable interval $\langle u - r, u + r \rangle$ around the calculated angle (or more precisely u position) are also incremented. That—unfortunately—introduces a new parameter of the method—radius r. However, experiments show that neither the robustness nor the speed is affected notably by the selection of r (except for the extreme cases).

The dependency of u on θ is not linear and thus the radius should vary for different u. However, the sensitivity of the algorithm to the radius is very low and the dependency is "close to linear" (see Fig. 6.1), so in practice, a constant "radius" is set in the u coordinate in the same way it is set for θ—experiments show that this does not cause any measurable error.

6.2 PClines on Graphics Processors (OpenGL)

The classical θ–ϱ Hough transform was implemented on graphical hardware by Diard [4] and Fung et. al. [5, 6], but the graphical hardware cannot directly rasterize sinusoid curves. Fung's implementation rasterizes the sinusoid curve as a polyline and Diard's implementation rasterizes several quad, that span across a larger portion of the parameter space. The PTLM parameterizations are more suitable for OpenGL implementation, because all modern graphical accelerators are capable of line rasterization.

The implementation of the HT using the $\mathcal{TS}$ parameterization is relatively straightforward. It uses OpenGL 3 features such as the *Geometry Shader*, *Geometry Instancing*, and *Transform Feedback*. The detection is composed of three separate stages done by the following shader programs:

- Image preprocessing program in case the input image requires preprocessing, namely conversion to grayscale. This program is optional.
- Accumulation program for accumulating the edges' votes from the input image to the $\mathcal{TS}$ space.
- Detection program for detecting local maxima in the $\mathcal{TS}$ space.

Both the image preprocessing and the $\mathcal{TS}$ space accumulation programs are implemented via rendering to a texture. The (optional) preprocessing step is done by simple screen quad rendering.

Most of the $\mathcal{TS}$ space accumulation is done by a geometry shader. A point for every pixel of the input image is rendered by geometry instancing. At first, built-in variables `gl_VertexID` and `gl_InstanceID` were used to specify the point coordinates. Unfortunately, on AMD (ATI) hardware, rendering of primitives with no attributes is not possible. Therefore, instead of `gl_VertexID`, the x coordinate is passed as a regular attribute by a vertex buffer object (VBO). Surprisingly, this performs faster even on NVIDIA hardware. The geometry shader reads the input image at the specified coordinates and thresholds the value to determine whether it is an edge. The output of the geometry shader is a three-point line strip that is rasterized to the $\mathcal{TS}$ space. The u coordinates of the points are fixed $\{-1, 0, 1\}$ and the v coordinates are based on the input point coordinates (x, y). The $\mathcal{TS}$ space is accumulated using additive blending into a floating-point texture.

The maxima detection is also performed by a geometry shader. A point is rendered for each pixel of the $\mathcal{TS}$ space (stored in the texture) and the geometry shader checks a small neighborhood of this pixel to see whether it is a local maximum. In that case, the detected line is returned by the *transform feedback*. The maxima detection could be implemented separably using two passes and one temporary texture. However,

Fig. 6.2 Three vertices used
for rendering two separate
line segments. The middle
point A_x has its z-coordinate
calculated as $(1 - r)/r$, where
r is the radius rendered around
the predicted u (this restricts
r to be smaller than d). The
depths of vertices A_{-y} and
A_y are calculated according
to the required lengths of the
line segments

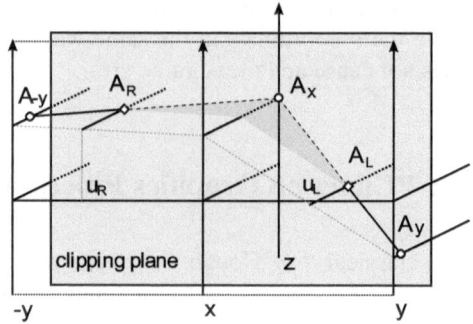

experiments have shown that the single pass detection performed faster for all used
neighborhood sizes.

When the detected edge gradient direction is taken into account, the algorithm
becomes only slightly complicated. Algorithm 6 shows the pseudocode of the geometry shader that performs the edge detection and emits the line segments for the
rasterization to the parameter space. Based on the orientation of the e.g., two or three
vertices are emitted. Although the $\mathcal{TS}$ space is a plane, 3D space is involved (lines
14–23). The third coordinate is used in one special case illustrated by Fig. 6.2. It is
the situation which occurs if the rendered part of the polyline around the estimated
u is outside of interval $[-d, d]$. Such a situation results in the necessity of rendering
two separate lines. Instead of calculating all four endpoints of the lines, only three
vertices are emitted with different z-coordinates and the back clipping plane of the
OpenGL view frustum is used to clip the polyline. This trick cannot be used, when
the rasterized portion of the line is larger than 50 % of the parameter space width,
but this is of no practical concern.

6.2.1 Experimental Results

This section presents the experimental evaluation of the presented OpenGL-based
algorithm.

The following hardware was used for testing (in bold face is the identifier used in
the text):

GTX 480 NVIDIA GTX 480 in a computer with Intel Core i7-920, 6 GB 3×DDR3-
1066(533 MHz) RAM;

GTX 280 NVIDIA GTX 280 in a computer with Intel Core i7-920, 6 GB 3×DDR3-
1066(533 MHz) RAM;

GT 130M NVIDIA GT 130 M mobile GPU in a laptop computer with Intel Core 2
DUO T6500, 2× 2 GB DDR2 399 MHz RAM;

Algorithm 6 Geometry Shader for Accumulation Using Edge Orientation

---

Input: Image I with dimensions W, H, radius r and $d=1$
Output: Accumulator space S
1: **for all** $x \in \{1, \ldots, W\}, y \in \{1, \ldots, H\}$ **do**
2:   $G_x = (I * S_x)(x, y)$
3:   $G_y = (I * S_y)(x, y)$
4:   $u = \dfrac{G_y}{G_x + \mathrm{sgn}(G_x)|G_y|}$
5:   **if** $G_x^2 + G_y^2 > \tau$ **then**
6:     $u_L = u + r, u_R = u - r$
7:     **if** $u_L <= 0 \wedge u_R <= 0$ **then**
8:       **emit vertex** $(u_L, u_L(y + x) + x, 0)$
9:       **emit vertex** $(u_R, u_R(y + x) + x, 0)$
10:     **else if** $u_L >= 0 \wedge u_R >= 0$ **then**
11:       **emit vertex** $(u_L, u_L(y - x) + x, 0)$
12:       **emit vertex** $(u_R, u_R(y - x) + x, 0)$
13:     **else if** $u_L < -1 \vee u_R > 1$ **then**
14:       **if** $u_L < -1$ **then**
15:         $u_L = u_L + 2$
16:       **end if**
17:       **if** $u_R > 1$ **then**
18:         $u_R = u_R - 2$
19:       **end if**
20:       $z = (1 - r)/r$
21:       **emit vertex** $(-1, -y, (z(1 + u_R) - 1)/u_R)$
22:       **emit vertex** $(0, x, z)$
23:       **emit vertex** $(1, y, (1 - z(1 - u_L))/u_L)$
24:     **else**
25:       **emit vertex** $(u_L, u_L(y + x) + x, 0)$
26:       **emit vertex** $(0, x, 0)$
27:       **emit vertex** $(u_R, u_R(y - x) + x, 0)$
28:     **end if**
29:   **end if**
30: **end for**

HD 5970-1 AMD Radeon HD5970 (single core used) in a computer with Intel Core i5-660, 4 GB 3×DDR3-1066(533 MHz) RAM;

HD 5970-2 AMD Radeon HD5970 (both cores used) in a computer with Intel Core i5-660, 4 GB 3×DDR3-1066(533 MHz) RAM; and

i7-920 Intel Core i7-920, 6 GB 3×DDR3-1066(533 MHz) RAM—the same computer is used for testing the GTX 480 and GTX 280.

The measurement was made on a randomly selected high-resolution real life images. The details of the experiment and a showcase of the dataset can be found in [1]. The presented algorithm (further referred to as **PClines**) was compared to a software implementation of the "standard" θ–ϱ based Hough transform taken from the **OpenCV** library[1] and parallelized by OpenMP and slightly optimized.

---

[1] http://opencv.willowgarage.com.

Fig. 6.3 Performance evaluation of computational complexity tested on real-world images. The GLSL implementation is compared to a parallelized OpenCV implementation (using all cores of the i7-920)

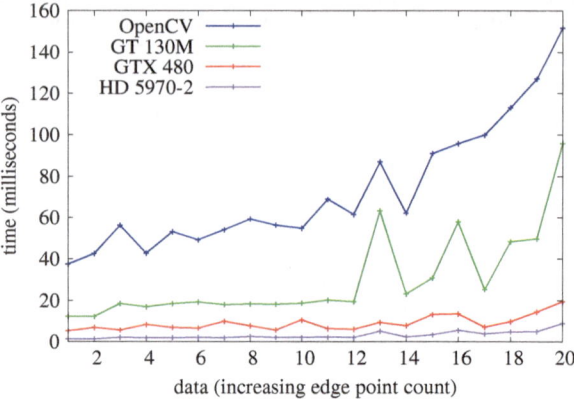

Fig. 6.4 Performance evaluation of the GLSL implementation using different high-end graphics hardware

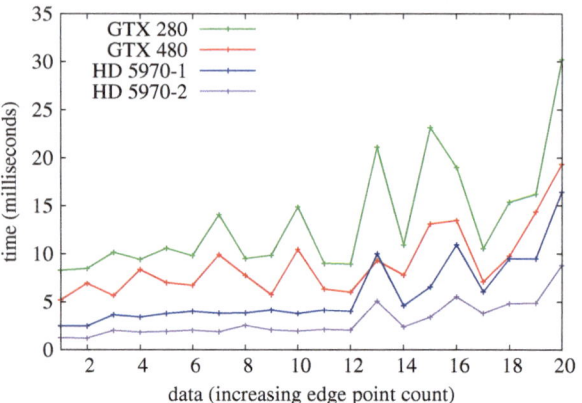

The results are reported in Fig. 6.3. The measurements verify that the computational complexity depends mostly on the number of edge points extracted from the input image and the edge-detection phase is linearly proportional to the image resolution, which causes the nonlinearities in the graph. The GPU-accelerated implementations are notably faster than the software implementation. A detailed comparison of the GPU-accelerated implementations is shown in Fig. 6.4. The graphs show that by using contemporary graphics chips, real-time processing can be achieved even for the "full" Hough transform, not relying on any randomized selection of the edges or sub-sampling of the Hough space.

6.3 Hough Transform on a Small Read-Write Memory

The classical Hough transform accesses sparsely a relatively large amount of memory. On some systems, such a large random-access read-write memory might be expensive or even not available at all. Even on systems with such memory, the sparse access can diminish the effect of caching. On CUDA and similar architectures, this effect is even more significant, as the global memory is not cached. To achieve real-time performance, the memory requirements must be limited to the *shared memory* of a multiprocessor (typically 16 kB).

Often, maxima in the parameter space are detected only locally from a small neighborhood. In such a case, the rest of the parameter space is not required even to exist at all. Josth et al. [7] presented a modified Hough transform that slides the parameter space by a window large enough for maxima detection but small enough to fit in the available memory. This modification was used for θ–ϱ and the PClines parameterizations, but only the PClines version will be described. The θ–ϱ version is very similar.

Algorithm 7 shows the modified Hough transform accumulation procedure. The key difference from the standard approach to accumulation is the actual size of the Hough space actively used at a time. The new algorithm stores only $n \times (v_{max} - v_{min})$ accumulators, where n is the neighborhood size required for the maxima detection. Values v_{min} and v_{max} define the discretization of the Hough space in the v axis; $v_{max} - v_{min}$ is the resolution in this axis. The u_{min} and u_{max} are the borders in the u axis, respectively.

Algorithm 7 HT accumulation strategy using a small read-write memory.

Input: Image I sized $W \times H$, neighborhood size n
Output: Detected lines $L = \{\ell_1, \dots\}$
1: $P \leftarrow \{(x, y) \in \{1, \dots, W\} \times \{1, \dots, H\}|$ at (x, y) is an edge in $I\}$
2: $S(i, v) \leftarrow 0, \forall i \in \{1, \dots, n\}, \forall v \in \{v_{min}, \dots, v_{max}\}$
3: **for all** $i \in \{1, \dots, n\}$ **do**
4:     **for all** $(x, y) \in P$ **do**
5:        **increment** $S(i, v(u_{min} + i - 1, x, y))$
6:     **end for**
7: **end for**
8: $L \leftarrow \{\}$
9: **for** $u = u_{min} + \lceil \frac{n}{2} \rceil - 1$ **to** $u_{max} - \lceil \frac{n}{2} \rceil$ **do**
10:    $L \leftarrow L \cup \{\ell(u, v)|v \in \{v_{min}, \dots, v_{max}\} \wedge$ at $(\lceil \frac{n}{2} \rceil, v)$ is a high local max. in $S\}$
11:    **for** $i = 1$ **to** $n - 1$ **do**
12:       $S(i, v) \leftarrow S(i + 1, v), \forall v \in \{v_{min}, \dots, v_{max}\}$
13:    **end for**
14:    $S(n, v) \leftarrow 0, \forall v \in \{v_{min}, \dots, v_{max}\}$
15:    **for all** $(x, y) \in P$ **do**
16:       **increment** $S(n, v(u + \lfloor \frac{n}{2} \rfloor, x, y))$
17:    **end for**
18: **end for**

Fig. 6.5 Illustration of
Algorithm 7. The *gray rectan-*
gle represents the buffer of *n*
columns. For column 4, the
above-threshold maxima are
detected in each step within
the buffer. Then, the column
7 values are accumulated into
the buffer, using the space of
column 2, which will not be
needed in future processing

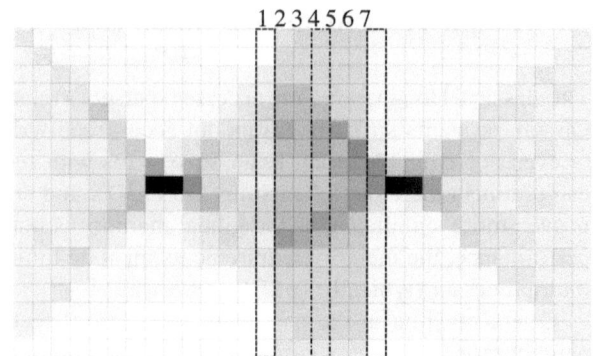

First, the detected edges are stored in a set P (line 1). Then, first n columns of the
Hough space are computed by lines 2–7. The memory necessary for containing the
n columns is all the read-write random-access memory required by the algorithm;
even for high resolutions of the Hough space, the buffer of n columns fits easily in
the *shared memory* of the GPU multiprocessors.

$S(i, v)$ is the discretized accumulator space—a buffer which is zeroed (lines 2
and 14), incremented (lines 5 and 16), and searched for maxima (line 10). Function
$v(u, x, y)$ computes the v coordinate based on the u coordinate and the point to be
accumulated (x, y):

$$u \in \mathcal{T} : v(u, x, y) = \frac{(x - y)u}{u_{\max}/2} + y,$$

$$u \in \mathcal{S} : v(u, x, y) = \frac{(y - x)u}{u_{\max}/2} + x, \tag{6.5}$$

In the main loop (lines 9–18), for every column of the Hough space the maxima
are detected (line 10), the accumulated neighborhood is shifted by one column (lines
11–13), and a new column is accumulated (lines 14–17); please refer to Fig. 6.5 for
an illustration of the algorithm. Thus, only the buffer of n columns is being reused.
The memory shift can be implemented using a circular buffer of lines to avoid data
copying. Also, in the actual implementation, pixels of one column follow each other
in the memory; this can be viewed as if the image was transposed.

In the pseudocode, maxima are not detected at the edges of the Hough space
(i.e. when $u \notin \{u_{\min} + \lceil \frac{n}{2} \rceil - 1, \ldots, u_{\max} - \lceil \frac{n}{2} \rceil\}$). Eventual handling of the
maxima detection at the edge of the Hough space does not change the algorithm
structure, but it would unnecessarily complicate the pseudocode. Two solutions
exist—either copying the border data or rasterizing necessary parts of the lines outside the Hough space. Both approaches perform similarly and their implementation is
straightforward.

On CUDA or OpenCL, the threads in a block can be used for processing the set of
edges P (lines 15–17 and 4–6) in parallel, by using an atomic increment of the shared

memory so as to avoid read-write collisions. In order to use all the multiprocessors of the GPU, the loop on line 9 is broken into a number (e.g. 90 is suitable for current NVIDIA GeForce graphics chips) of sub-loops processed by individual blocks of threads.

The algorithm as described above uses exactly $n \times (v_{max} - v_{min})$ memory cells, typically 16-bit integer values. In cases where the runtime system has a higher amount of fast random-access read-write memory, this memory can be used fully; and instead of accumulating one column of the Hough space (lines 15–17 of the algorithm), several columns are processed at a time, and more than one column is searched for maxima by line 10. This leads to a further speedup by reducing the number of steps carried out by the loop over u (line 9).

6.3.1 Harnessing the Edge Orientation

The approach for utilizing the detected gradient from Sect. 6.1 can be incorporated into the new accumulation scheme presented here. When extracting the "edge points" for which the two lines are accumulated in the $\mathcal{TS}$ space (line 1 in Algorithm 7), the edge inclination is also extracted:

1: $P \leftarrow \{(\alpha, x, y) | x \in \{1, \ldots, W\} \wedge y \in \{1, \ldots, H\}$

$\wedge$ at (x, y) is an edge in I with gradient slope $\alpha\}$.

Then, instead of accumulating all points from set P (lines 4–6), only those points which fall into the interval with radius w around currently processed θ are processed and accumulated into the buffer of n lines:

4: **for all**$(\alpha, x, y) \in P \wedge i - w < u(\alpha) < i + w$ **do**
5:     **increment** $S(i, v(i, x, y))$
6: **end for**

and similarly for lines 15–17.

It should be noted that the edge extraction phase (line 1) can sort the detected edges by their gradient inclination α, so that loops on lines 15–17 and 4–6 do not visit all edges, but only edges potentially accumulated, based on the current u (line 9 of Algorithm 7). For (partially) sorting the edges on GPU, an efficient prefix sum can be used [8].

6.3.2 Experimental Results

This section presents the experimental evaluation of the presented algorithm implemented for CUDA. Section 6.2 describes a PClines-based algorithm for OpenGL which is used as a reference in the measurements.

The following hardware was used for testing (in bold face is the identifier used later on in this text):

GTX 480 NVIDIA GTX 480 in a computer with Intel Core i7-920, 6 GB 3×DDR3-1066(533 MHz) RAM;

GTX 280 NVIDIA GTX 280 in a computer with Intel Core i7-920, 6 GB 3×DDR3-1066(533 MHz) RAM;

HD 5970-1 AMD Radeon HD5970 (single core used) in a computer with Intel Core i5-660, 4 GB 3×DDR3-1066(533 MHz) RAM;

HD 5970-2 AMD Radeon HD5970 (both cores used) in a computer with Intel Core i5-660, 4 GB 3×DDR3-1066(533 MHz) RAM; and

i7-920 Intel Core i7-920, 6 GB 3×DDR3-1066(533 MHz) RAM—the same computer is used for testing the GTX 480 and GTX 280.

Performance Evaluation on Real-Life Images

Two datasets were used for measuring the performance of different algorithms. The first one was a set of real photographs with different amounts of edge points and different dimensions—see Fig. 6.6. The images are sorted according to the number of edge points detected by the Sobel filter. Only this limited set of images is selected for the graphs to be readable. The images were selected randomly from a large set of images and they well represent the behavior of the algorithms for all images we have observed.

The presented algorithm (referred to below as **PClines-CUDA**) was compared to different alternatives:

- A software implementation of the PClines based on a Hough transform implementation taken from the **OpenCV** library[2] and parallelized by OpenMP and slightly optimized.
- A CUDA implementation of the standard θ–ϱ parameterization (**ThetaRho-CUDA**). The arrangement of the algorithm is very similar to the presented PClines-based one.
- The OpenGL implementation of PClines (**PClines-OpenGL**) as described in Sect. 6.2.

The results on the set of high-resolution real-life images are shown in Fig. 6.7. The measurements verify that the computational complexity is linearly proportional to the number of edge points extracted from the input image and the edge-detection phase is linearly proportional to the image resolution. The GPU-accelerated implementations are notably faster than the software implementation. A detailed comparison of the GPU-accelerated implementations is shown in Fig. 6.8.

---

[2] http://opencv.willowgarage.com.

Fig. 6.6: Images used in the test. The number in the *top-left* corner of each thumbnail image is the image ID—used on the horizontal axis in Figs. 6.7 and 6.8. The *bottom-left* corner of each thumbnail image states the pixel resolution of the tested image

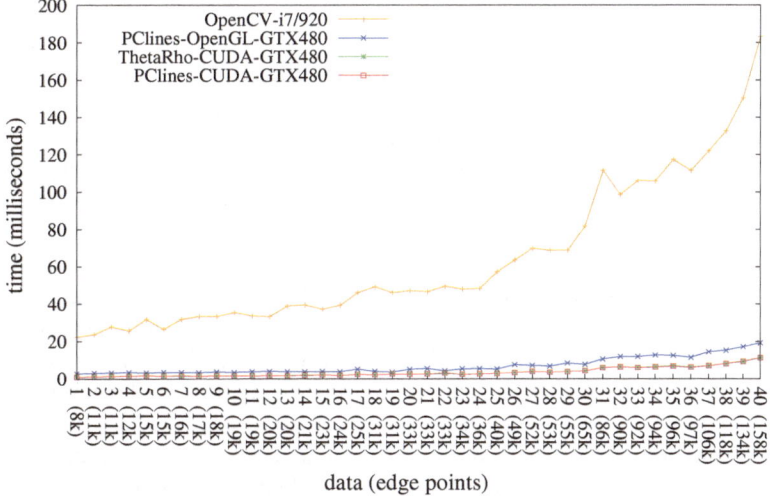

Fig. 6.7: Performance evaluation on real-world images (see Fig. 6.6) using the Sobel operator and only accumulating an interval on the *u* axis (Sect. 6.3.1)

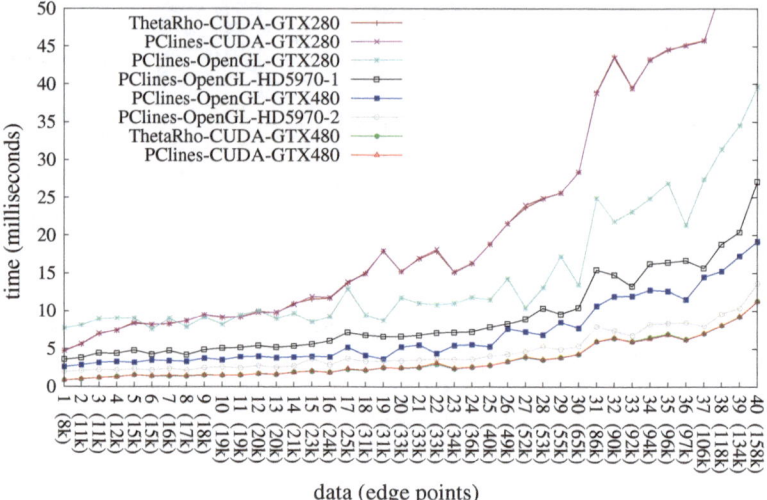

Fig. 6.8: Performance evaluation on real-world images (see Fig. 6.6) using the Sobel operator and only accumulating an interval on the u axis (Sect. 6.3.1). Only the hardware-accelerated methods are shown here for better clarity

Performance Evaluation on Synthetic Binary Images

The second dataset consisted of automatically generated black-and-white images. The generator randomly places L white lines in an originally black image and then inverts pixels on P random positions in the image. The evaluation is done on 36 images (resolution 1600×1200): images 1–6, 7–12, 13–18, 19–24, 25–30, 31–36 are generated with $L = 1, 30, 60, 90, 120, 150$, respectively, with increasing $P = 1, 3000, 6000, 9000, 12000$ for each L. The suitable parameters for images of these properties were $H_\varrho = 960$ and $H_\theta = 1170$ (resolution of the Hough space) and the threshold for accumulators in the Hough space was 400. The purpose of this test was to accurately observe the dependency of processing time on the number of lines in the image and on the number of pixels processed as edges. These two quantities determine the number of repetitions in the critical parts of the algorithm.

Figure 6.9 shows the results of the four implementations; Fig. 6.10 contains a selection of the graphs—only the hardware-accelerated methods. Once again, it should be noted that all the accelerated versions are several times faster than the commonly used OpenCV implementation and achieve real-time or near real-time speeds even for high-resolution inputs.

On current graphics chips, the algorithm presented here (PClines-CUDA) and the previously published algorithm (ThetaRho-CUDA) perform equally fast (it should be noted that in Figs. 6.8 and 6.10 their curves totally overlap). On special, embedded, and low-power architectures, the PClines-based version may perform much better or can be the only feasible one. That is because it requires no floating-point computations

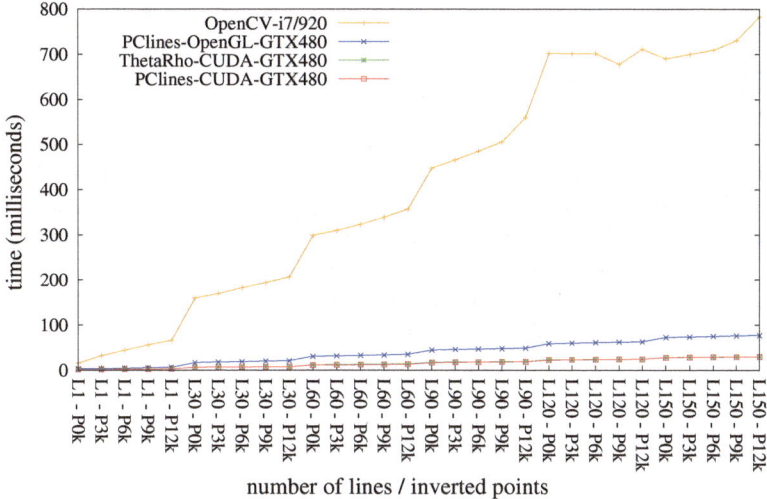

Fig. 6.9: Performance evaluation on generated data

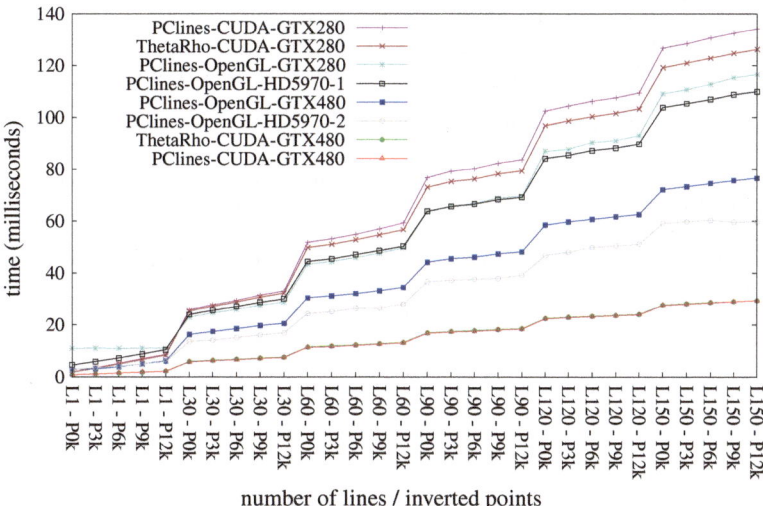

Fig. 6.10: Performance evaluation on generated data. Only the hardware-accelerated methods are shown here for better clarity

and no goniometric functions (which are cheaply available on the GPUs). The only advantages of the PClines-based algorithm on GPU is, therefore, its better accuracy [9] and its ability to directly detect parallel lines and sets of lines coincident with one point.

Figures 6.8 and 6.10 show that on the Fermi NVIDIA card (GTX280) the OpenGL version of the PClines-based Hough transform performs better than CUDA. Very good results also come from recent Radeon graphics chips (with the OpenGL version). The Fermi architecture (compared to the previous generation) did not speed up the algorithm in the OpenGL version as much as the CUDA implementation. For weaker graphics chips (low-power, mobile, etc.), the OpenGL version of the PClines-based algorithm might be the right choice.

References

1. Dubská, M., Havel, J., Herout, A.: Real-time detection of lines using parallel coordinates and OpenGL. In: Proceedings of SCCG (2011)
2. O'Gorman, F., Clowes, M.B.: Finding picture edges through collinearity of feature points. IEEE Trans. Comput. 25(4), 449–456 (1976)
3. Shapiro, L.G.: Stockman, G.C.: Computer Vision. Tom Robbins, Prentice Hall (2001)
4. Diard, F.: Using the Geometry Shader for Compact and Variable-Length GPU Feedback, In: GUP Gems 3, Chap. 41. Addison-Wesley, Botson (2008)
5. Fung, J., Mann, S., Aimone, C.: Openvidia: parallel gpu computer vision. In: Proceedings of the 13th Annual ACM International Conference on Multimedia, MULTIMEDIA '05, pp. 849–852. ACM, New York (2005)
6. Fung, J.: Computer Vision on the GPU, In: GPU Gems, Chap. 40. Addison-Wesley, Boston (2005)
7. Jošth, R., Dubská, M., Herout, A., Havel, J.: Real-time line detection using accelerated high-resolution Hough transform. In: Proceedings of Scandinavian Conference on Image Analysis (SCIA) (2011)
8. Harris, M.: Parallel Prefix Sum (Scan) with CUDA, In: GPU Gems 3, Chap. 39. Addison-Wesley, Boston (2007)
9. Dubská, M., Herout, A., Havel, J.: PClines—line detection using parallel coordinates. In: Proceedings of CVPR (2011)

Chapter 7
Conclusion

This text briefly captures existing information about the Hough transform and its usability for detecting grids and pencils of projected parallel lines. We described in detail the role of the point-to-line mappings in detection of such structures. Various point-to-line mappings can serve as suitable parameterizations for the Hough transform.

We were presenting one particular point-to-line mapping—the PClines—as an intuitive representative of this set. This parameterization offers both low discretization error and computational efficiency. Since PClines is a point-to-line mapping, vanishing points are represented by lines. This allows for straightforward detection of the vanishing points, and by using the cross-ratio and its manifestation in the parameter space, regularly spaced lines can be efficiently detected as well. This allows for detection of grids, such as different calibration checker-board patterns or matrix codes (QR code and similar).

We summarized the possibilities of implementing the PClines (and other PTLM-based HT variants) on contemporary graphics chips. These results show that by using the PClines parameterization, even high-resolution images can be processed and searched for lines and grids in real time.

A. Herout et al., *Real-Time Detection of Lines and Grids*,
SpringerBriefs in Computer Science, DOI: 10.1007/978-1-4471-4414-4_7,
© Adam Herout 2013

Appendix A
PClines Octave Implementation

Octave version 3.6.x and octave-forge package is required.

```
% main function "pclines"
%
%   [I,u,v] = pclines(src, N);
%
% input:
%   src - A matrix with edge pixels for accumulation equal to 0
%   N   - A number of lines which have to be detected
%
% output:
%   pairs of theta-rho parameters for detected lines
function [H, theta, rho] = pclines(src, N)
  % space initialization
  S = size(src);
  SpaceSize = [max(S),max(S)*2];
  H = zeros(SpaceSize);

  [y,x] = find(src == 0);  % edge points extraction

  x -= (S(2)/2); % coordinate system translation
  y -= (S(1)/2); % origin is now in the middle of the image

  H = rasterizeTSspace(x(:),y(:),H); % call TSspace rasterization
  thresh = sqrt(S*S')/4; %threshold for maxima detection
  [u,v] = findMaxima(H, N, thresh);
  [theta, rho] = lineParameters(u,v,SpaceSize) %conversion to
      line parameters
end

% two pass rasterization
function [H] = rasterizeTSspace(X,Y,H)
  H = rasterHalf(X, Y, H, 1, 0); % S space accumulation

  offset = size(H,2)/2 - 1; % offset for second half
  H = rasterHalf(Y, -X + 1, H, 2, offset); % T space accumulation
end
```

A. Herout et al., *Real-Time Detection of Lines and Grids*,
SpringerBriefs in Computer Science, DOI: 10.1007/978-1-4471-4414-4,
© Adam Herout 2013

```
% rasterization of a one part (S or T) of Hough space
function [H] = rasterHalf(X, Y, H, start, offset)
  L = linspace(X,Y,size(H,2)/2); % line rasterization

  for i = 1:size(L,1)
    row = L(i,:) + size(H,1)/2;

    for j = start:size(L,2)
      H(round(row(j)), j + offset) += 1;   % accumulation
    end
  end
end

% maxima detection
function[u,v] = findMaxima(H, N, thresh)
  [v,u,w] = immaximas(H, 3, thresh); % maxima detection

  if (length(w) == 0)
    return;
  end

  [tmp,i] = sort(w,'descend'); % sorting

  count = min(length(w), N);
  u = u(i(1:count)); % take N or less highest maxima
  v = v(i(1:count));
end


% line parameters
function[theta,rho] = lineParameters(u, v, S)
  d = S(2)/2;
  u = d - u; % move origin to the center of the space
  v = v - S(1)/2;

  % transformation to line parameters
  theta = atan2(d - abs(u), u);
  rho = (v.*d./(d - abs(u))).*sin(theta);
end
```

Listing A.1 PClines

Appendix B
Cross-Ratio in Matrix Form

The input are coordinates of the points $\mathbf{a}, \mathbf{b}, \mathbf{c}$ and their indices a, b, c in the sequences of perspectively projected parallel equidistant lines in Parallel coordinates. The problem is to find point $\mathbf{d}$ with a given index n. The equation results from the expression of $\mathbf{d}$ in the (5.16).

$$(\alpha\,\beta\,0) = (a\,b\,c)\begin{pmatrix} (b-n) & 0 & 0 \\ 0 & (a-n) & 0 \\ (n-b) & (n-a) & 0 \end{pmatrix} \tag{B.1}$$

The coordinates of the point $\mathbf{d}$ can then be calculated as in Eq. (B.2).

$$\mathbf{d} = (\mathbf{d}_1, \mathbf{d}_2, \mathbf{d}_3)$$

$$\mathbf{d}_i = \frac{(\alpha\,\beta\,0)\cdot((\mathbf{b}_i\,\mathbf{a}_i\,\mathbf{b}_i)\times(\mathbf{a}_i\,\mathbf{a}_i\,\mathbf{c}_i))}{(\alpha\,\beta\,0)\cdot((1\,1\,1)\times(\mathbf{a}_i\,\mathbf{b}_i\,\mathbf{c}_i))} = \frac{\begin{vmatrix} \alpha & \beta & 0 \\ \mathbf{b}_i & \mathbf{a}_i & \mathbf{b}_i \\ \mathbf{a}_i & \mathbf{a}_i & \mathbf{c}_i \end{vmatrix}}{\begin{vmatrix} \alpha & \beta & 0 \\ 1 & 1 & 1 \\ \mathbf{a}_i & \mathbf{b}_i & \mathbf{c}_i \end{vmatrix}} \tag{B.2}$$

A. Herout et al., *Real-Time Detection of Lines and Grids*,
SpringerBriefs in Computer Science, DOI: 10.1007/978-1-4471-4414-4,
© Adam Herout 2013

Appendix C
Horizon Orientation and Resampling Function

This appendix derives the Eqs. (5.20) and (5.22) in Sect. 5.4.2. The proof is given for the S space, but the equations for the T space can be calculated in the same way. Also, only the proof for u_i from Eq. (5.22) is provided because for v_i the proof is identical.

Let us start with perspectively projected lines with the horizon parallel to the x-axis. Because of parallelism, the intersection on axis x are equidistant, and the ordered set of lines can be defined as follows:

$$\ell_0 : x = m_0 y + b_0$$
$$\ell_1 : x = m_1 y + (b_0 + t)$$
$$\ldots \tag{C.1}$$
$$\ell_n : x = m_n y + (b_0 + nt)$$

The lines' slopes in the ordered set (C.1) can be defined recursively:

$$m_n = \frac{x - (b_0 + nt)}{y}$$
$$m_n = nm_1 - (n - 1)m_0 \tag{C.2}$$

However, the horizon can have an arbitrary orientation in Fig. C.1. Equation (C.3) defines how the *slope* of the line has changed when the *inclination* θ changed by a rotation angle α.

$$\theta = \arctan(-m)$$
$$\theta' = \theta + \alpha = \arctan(-m) + \alpha \tag{C.3}$$
$$m' = -\tan \theta' = \frac{m - \tan \alpha}{1 + m \tan \alpha}$$

For an inverse mapping, two fixed points in PC (lines from a projected parallel lines) are needed (see Sect. 5.4.2).

A. Herout et al., *Real-Time Detection of Lines and Grids*,
SpringerBriefs in Computer Science, DOI: 10.1007/978-1-4471-4414-4,
© Adam Herout 2013

Fig. C.1 Angles in horizon orientation

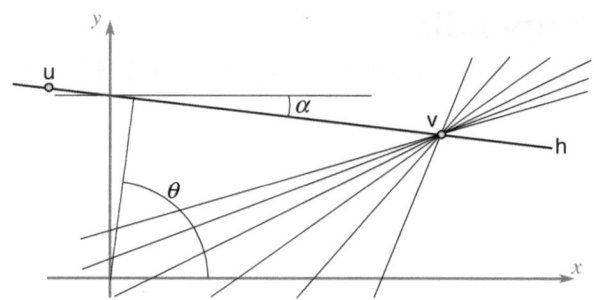

$$\bar{l}_0 : (u_0, v_0, 1)_{\mathbb{P}^2}$$
$$\bar{l}_1 : (u_1, v_1, 1)_{\mathbb{P}^2} \tag{C.4}$$

Their slopes are defined by the coordinates in the Parallel system. In the Cartesian coordinates, the rotation is done for the right orientation of the horizon.

$$m_0 = \frac{u_0}{u_0 - d}, \quad m_1 = \frac{u_1}{u_1 - d}$$

$$m_0' = \frac{m_0 - \tan \alpha}{1 + m_0 \tan \alpha} \tag{C.5}$$
$$m_1' = \frac{m_1 - \tan \alpha}{1 + m_1 \tan \alpha}$$

The slope of an arbitrary line from the ordered set can be derived using (C.2).

$$m_n' = nm_1' - (n - 1)m_0'$$
$$m_n = \frac{m_n' - \tan(-\alpha)}{1 + m_n' \tan(-\alpha)} = \frac{m_n' + \tan \alpha}{1 - m_n' \tan \alpha}, \tag{C.6}$$

From a line-to-point mapping between the Cartesian and parallel coordinates, the u position of $\bar{\mathbf{p}}_n$ is a function of m_n and by substitution of (C.6), (C.5), (C.3), and (C.2) the result is as follows:

$$u_n = \frac{m_n d}{m_n - 1}$$
$$u_n = \frac{(-\tan \alpha - 1)u_1 u_0 + d(nu_1 - (n-1)u_0)}{(-\tan \alpha - 1)(nu_0 - (n-1)u_1) + d}. \tag{C.7}$$

Angle α of the rotation can be derived from detected lines $\bar{\mathbf{u}}$ and $\bar{\mathbf{v}}$ in the parallel coordinates representing the vanishing points $\mathbf{u}$ and $\mathbf{v}$ in the Cartesian coordinates. They define the horizon line: their intersection in parallel coordinates (i.e. their common line in CC).

$$\bar{\mathbf{u}} = \mathbf{l}_u = (-1, m_u, b_u)_{\mathbb{P}^2}$$
$$\bar{\mathbf{v}} = \mathbf{l}_v = (-1, m_v, b_v)_{\mathbb{P}^2}$$
$$\bar{\mathbf{h}} = (-1, m_u, b_u)_{\mathbb{P}^2} \times (-1, m_v, b_v)_{\mathbb{P}^2}$$
$$= (m_u b_v - m_v b_u, b_v - b_u, m_u - m_v)_{\mathbb{P}^2}$$
(C.8)

The parameters of the horizon line in the Cartesian coordinates are as in Eq. (C.9).

$$\mathbf{h} = ((m_u - m_v)d - (m_u b_v - m_v b_u), m_u b_v - m_v b_u, (b_u - b_v)d)_{\mathbb{P}^2}$$
$$\mathbf{h} = (\cos\theta, \sin\theta, \rho)_{\mathbb{P}^2}$$
(C.9)

$$\tan\alpha = \tan(\frac{\pi}{2} - \theta) = \cot\theta = \frac{\cos\theta}{\sin\theta}$$
$$\tan\alpha = \frac{(m_u - m_v)d - (m_u b_v - m_v b_u)}{m_u b_v - m_v b_u}$$
$$\tan\alpha = \frac{\begin{vmatrix} m_u & m_v & 0 \\ 1 & 1 & 1 \\ b_u & b_v & d \end{vmatrix}}{\begin{vmatrix} m_u & m_v \\ b_u & b_v \end{vmatrix}}$$
(C.10)

Appendix D
Proof of the Equation for the Grid Lines

A line of the grid is specified by its two points with $t_0 \neq t_1$ as

$$\mathbf{l}_u(i) = \mathbf{p}_u(i, t_0) \times \mathbf{p}_u(i, t_1). \tag{D.1}$$

By expanding according to Eq. (5.4) and reordering, a part of the point equation that depends on t is isolated

$$\mathbf{l}_u(i) = (\mathbf{p}_0 + \text{step}_s(i)\mathbf{u} + t_0\mathbf{v}) \times (\mathbf{p}_0 + \text{step}_s(i)\mathbf{u} + t_1\mathbf{v}) \tag{D.2}$$

$$= (\mathbf{p}_u(i, 0) + t_0\mathbf{v}) \times (\mathbf{p}_u(i, 0) + t_1\mathbf{v}) \tag{D.3}$$

The cross product is distributive over addition, so

$$\mathbf{l}_u(i) = (\mathbf{p}_u(i, 0) + t_0\mathbf{v}) \times \mathbf{p}_u(i, 0) + (\mathbf{p}_u(i, 0) + t_0\mathbf{v}) \times t_1\mathbf{v} \tag{D.4}$$

$$= \mathbf{p}_u(i, 0) \times \mathbf{p}_u(i, 0) + t_0\mathbf{v} \times \mathbf{p}_u(i, 0) + \mathbf{p}_u(i, 0) \times t_1\mathbf{v} + t_0\mathbf{v} \times t_1\mathbf{v} \tag{D.5}$$

Due to the cross product anticommutativity ($a \times b = -b \times a$) and alternativity ($a \times a = 0$),

$$\mathbf{l}_u(i) = 0 + (t_1 - t_0)\mathbf{p}_u(i, 0) \times \mathbf{v} + 0 \tag{D.6}$$

$$= (t_1 - t_0)(\mathbf{p}_0 + \text{step}_s(i)\mathbf{u}) \times \mathbf{v}. \tag{D.7}$$

Distributing the cross product again reorders the equation to the weighted sum of the "first" line and the horizon

$$\mathbf{l}_u(i) = (t_1 - t_0)(\mathbf{p}_0 \times \mathbf{v} + \text{step}_s(i)\mathbf{u} \times \mathbf{v}) \tag{D.8}$$

$$= (t_1 - t_0)(\mathbf{l}_u^0 + \text{step}_s(i)\mathbf{l}^\infty). \tag{D.9}$$

A. Herout et al., *Real-Time Detection of Lines and Grids*,
SpringerBriefs in Computer Science, DOI: 10.1007/978-1-4471-4414-4,
© Adam Herout 2013

Index

A. Herout et al., *Real-Time Detection of Lines and Grids*,
SpringerBriefs in Computer Science, DOI: 10.1007/978-1-4471-4414-4,
© Adam Herout 2013